*w*est marin re*vi*ew

2018

08

A Publishing Collaboration

NEIGHBORS & FRIENDS

POINT REYES BOOKS

BLACK MOUNTAIN CIRCLE

PROSE

POETRY

ABOVE Christa Burgoyne, *Small Barn*, 2016, watercolor, 5⅜ × 6 inches
FRONT COVER Kay Bradner, *Ten Birds* (detail), 2017, oil on aluminum, 30 × 31½ inches.
Courtesy of Seager Gray Gallery, Mill Valley, California

ART + ARTIFACT

west marin review

Yes—I want to support this award-winning literary and art journal!

PLEASE ACCEPT MY DONATION OF:

☐ $50   ☐ $100   ☐ $250   ☐ $1,000   OTHER $ _____

☐ CHECK: Please make payable to *West Marin Review*

☐ VISA   ☐ MASTER CARD

_____
CREDIT CARD NO.   EXPIRES

_____
SIGNATURE

_____
NAME

_____
ADDRESS

_____
CITY   STATE   ZIP

_____
PHONE   E-MAIL

Thank you for your tax-deductible contribution.

westmarinreview.org

Your stamp helps
support community
publishing.

west marin re*view*

Post Office Box 1302
Point Reyes Station, California 94956

Dear Reader

WELCOME BACK to the *West Marin Review*, and to Volume number 8, a publishing collaboration of Neighbors and Friends—all volunteer designers and editors—with Point Reyes Books and Black Mountain Circle.

This fine literary journal is defined to a great degree by the diversity of its contributors. These are writers and artists who come not only from West Marin, here on the edge of the San Francisco Bay Area, but also from around the world. They range in age from five to ninety-five. Some are many-times-published professional writers and artists, and an equal number are seeing their work in print for the first thrilling time.

Diversity extends to content as well. The *Review* features fiction and nonfiction, poetry, sometimes music, and high-quality reproductions of every kind of visual art in every medium, meriting several design awards. Through the magic of our design team, art often becomes a transformative element alongside prose or poetry. That alchemy, the artful combination of extraordinary visuals and excellent writing, creates something more lasting, more profound than the art and the words alone. In this volume, you'll see the effect of Susan Hall's *California Twilight* and Sandy White's *Roy's Redwoods* bookending cowboy Dave Stamey's story, "Steelhead Lake." Feel/see the emotional resonance in May Ta's *Somber Summer* and "the long way to wander" in Thomas Hickey's "Monk's Empty Eye."

Though the *Review* does not publish to a theme as many journals do, it sometimes happens that a theme emerges among the many hundreds of pieces of art, poetry, and prose we consider for

Lissa Nicolaus, *Country Road*, 2010,
oil on canvas, 14 × 11 inches

each volume. This year, it was eerily so. Some of the most powerful submissions in every category referred to dark times, past and present. Former U.S. Poet Laureate Robert Hass's poem, "DANCING," roils with a historical saga of violence almost from the beginning of time right up to a nightclub in Orlando. Prartho Sereno's "Emergency Lock-Down Drill" is a stunning prose poem for these times. Michel Venghiattis and Richard Kirschman each offer documentary photo essays that remind us of war in Europe in the 1940s and the Troubles in Ireland in 1969. And though the prose readers selected it without knowing what poetry or art would be chosen for this volume, the featured long fiction, Molly Giles's "Next Time," introduces us to a father and daughter touring World War II battlefields.

Many more coincidences abound in this volume, along with extraordinary art that illuminates the pages, much as Kay Bradner's *Ten Birds* and sun-struck trees brighten the cover. (Birds could be another theme, if one were looking. Between the two covers on which sixteen birds perch, see if you can find "goldfinch and grace," a "peregrine promise," parrots and osprey, starlings and vultures, a blue heron, a waking owl. And look for Cathy Rose's porcelain doves, Isis Hockenos's excellent chickens, Jon Ching's amazing macaw, Xander Weaver-Scull's Arctic falcons, and thank you, Lily Andrews, for the hummingbird.)

Now, Dear Reader, may we ask: If you are touched by this volume, if it provokes reflection, if it inspires or simply entertains you, please use the envelope provided in this book to send us a donation. Your support allows us to continue publishing, with all that it means to the writers and artists featured here, and to all readers, like you, of the *West Marin Review*.

POEM Tobi Earnheart-Gold, "Untitled"
ART Kimberly Carr Harmon, *Wooded Gate*,
2015, digital photograph

We had prepared for all contingencies.
When we arrived the gate was open.
It became apparent to many of us
the gate had always been open:
the one contingency we had failed to plan for.

Between Birth and Song

Mary Winegarden

Between wild and tamed,
lyrical and lonely, the spoken and unnamed.

Must I now choose between silver and salt,
goldfinch and grace, blame and default?

Between blossom and bloom,
high tide, high noon?

Let me trespass from forgiveness to fire,
from chalk to caress, defeat to high wire.

Let me reclaim both aspen and duty,
syntax and sorrow, dark blue and beauty.

Emmeline Craig, *Living on the Edge* (detail), 2016, water-mixable oil on canvas, 24 × 48 inches

Bolinas Bound

Jackie Garcia Mann

MOUNT TAM: *At 5:13 p.m. someone watched a man barefoot,*
shirtless and dressed in white jeans, exit his car and walk
down the middle of the road, gazing up at the trees.
—*Point Reyes Light*, "Sheriff's Calls," August 13, 2015

BRYAN IS walking barefoot, shirtless, and dressed in white jeans
down the double yellow. He is gazing up at the treetops along
Panoramic Highway. Paula has disappeared and now they're going
to be late for dinner. He should probably be more worried about her,
but he is distracted by the dramatic view.

They have just left a hot, sunny afternoon in Sausalito. The
day's heat has been whisked away by the offshore flow, and the fog
is blowing in hard on the west side of Mount Tam. White clouds
unroll over the mountaintops, tucking the redwoods under a bedtime
marine blanket. Bryan had left his dirty blue van at the last pullout
when he got out to take a leak. He doesn't care that cars are honking
at him. The view is better from the middle of the road.

"Get out of the road, you idiot," a guy shouts from a passing car.

Bryan flips him the bird. He is only slightly stoned. The boy
who works at the kayak rental place had given him two pot cookies
at lunch. He seemed like a cool kid, not as uptight as his own teenage
son. The kid said he had an M-card for anxiety, like everyone else in
the county nowadays. The weed sure made his time working on the
street corner pass by faster.

"Totally beautiful." Bryan spins in a circle. The rivers of fog
are swallowing the deep green hillsides. He was raised on the coast in

Bolinas, and after fifty years he still never tires of watching the tidal waves of fog advance and recede over the coastal hills.

Maybe he shouldn't have had that second cookie before driving home.

"Paula! Come back, Paula!" Bryan yells out. He doesn't want to look anymore and he's hungry. Hell, he's going to take a nap and wait her out. She's a smart girl. The air feels clammy against his sunburned shoulders.

Molly and Pedro are hanging in the van, totally unconcerned about Paula. Some friends.

"We're just gonna chill here for a while, dudes," Bryan slides open the door.

"Cool man," Pedro nods and settles in for a nap. Molly blinks and goes back to sleep.

They are tired after working all day. Pedro and Molly doze off, but Bryan is too high to sleep. Then he hears her. He throws on a jacket and wades outside into the fog.

"Paula? Where are you, Paula?" Bryan cups his hands together and shouts. He hears her call back from the steep slope behind the van. Damn. He'll have to go after her.

What shitty luck, to step out into that wind when he got out to take a piss. He should have known better. He starts climbing up through the redwood duff and crumbling rocks, intensely aware of the redwood needles beneath his hands. He puts his nose to the ground like a dog and smells. It smells like redwoody mushrooms or maybe mushroomy redwoods. It smells deeply good, a spicy, earthy umami. When he was a kid, he went chanterelle hunting a few times up on Mount Tam with some of his mother's friends. He used to think he'd grow up to be a park ranger and lead nature walks. A lot of things hadn't worked out like he'd hoped. But it wasn't so bad, running his little sidewalk show. He liked being outside, talking to people all day.

"Yoo-hoo! Hey baby!" Paula is screeching. She isn't very far from the road.

What a drama queen. "Paula get your ass down here!"

"Hello, hello! Peek-a-boo. Peek-a-boo," she calls from up in a tree.

"I found you, girl!" Bryan spots her halfway up a redwood. Thank God, now they can get going.

Paula's blue feathers blend surprisingly well with the green foliage, but her bright yellow chest flashes like a beacon in the gray light. Bryan digs out a monkey chow pellet from his jeans pocket and holds it up so Paula can see the treat.

Paula bobs up and down shouting, "I love you. I love you." The macaw clumsily drops down through the branches to his arm. She takes the biscuit gently with her foot and bends her head for some petting. Bryan gives her bill a squeeze and reassures her with a few scritches on the nape of her neck. She chatters anxiously on the way to the van. He moves her onto his shoulder and her claws dig into him extra tight.

"Yah, scary as shit, wasn't it, big girl?" When Bryan stepped out to pee, the updraft from the fog had ripped Paula off his shoulder and sent her sailing like a kite into the sky. The bird didn't know what to do; her wings were clipped. She talked and posed for photos better than she flew.

"You're a smart cookie, Paula. Hella smart." Bryan puts Paula on her perch next to Molly and Pedro, his feathered family, who pose for photos with tourists on the Sausalito sidewalk.

Bryan the Birdman, people called him. He liked the name. It made him feel famous, like that Birdman of Alcatraz. Only he was better off than that dude because at least he wasn't spending his life on The Rock. Maybe he hadn't amounted to much, but his parrot photos are in thousands of vacation albums around the world. He's practically a TripAdvisor celebrity in China and Japan and he's never even left home. That's something.

Bryan starts up the VW's engine and pulls onto the serpentine road. He is Bolinas bound. They'll be late for Sunday dinner at his mom's house.

"Hey, Paulie Girl, you flew! You're like a wild parrot. You're a *Free Bird!*" Bryan bellows the words to the song: *If I leave here tomorrow, would you still remember me? For I must be travelin' on now, there's too many places I got to see….*

Christa Burgoyne, *Late Afternoon "C" Street*, 2016, watercolor, 7½ × 11 inches

Leaving for Italy

Michael Sykes

THE LONG train of forgetting was about to leave the station. All my friends and lovers had come to see me off. They mingled among themselves, passing the time of day, chatting amiably.

Far off in the distance a wildcat did growl: two riders were approaching—the wind, the wind!

"My God, we're leaving it all behind!"

I sat with my luggage in a stone courtyard next to the conductor's quarters, my feet propped on a small valise. A hummingbird came to a wall hung with a cascade of vines and flowers, hovering in the fluid sunshine before the open blossoms, its delicate beak dipping into the center for only the briefest moment. Then it flew away again.

I felt an ache of the purest joy and sadness rising in my heart, like a great upwelling at sea of nutrient-rich water caused by the shifting of ocean currents. Now animals rarely seen in these waters began arriving day after day, strange, wonderful creatures, like the majestic leatherback turtle that cruised slowly into view, its great bulk passing like the shadow of a cloud, trailing wide, lazy flippers as it drifted through a school of silvery fish.

I heard someone say: "It must be El Niño."

"It is El Niño!" someone cried.

"El Niño!"

She came in and sat on the bench beside me.

"It's time to go," she said.

"But how can I leave," I said, looking into the garden of the courtyard. "Who will take care of this garden? It needs work. There's still so much to be done."

"It will take care of itself," she said.

I looked at the tangle of luxuriant growth, all the weeds mixed in with exotic plants and ferns, masses of flowering shrubs and vines, all of it teeming with a rich fecundity that confused and delighted me at once. I felt my connection with this garden, this interior court-yard, the stone walls adorned with flowers, once again like the ache in my heart that was spreading throughout the great cavity of my chest, filling all the far-off corners.

"But how can I remember it all?" I asked. "There's too much."

"You won't need to," she said. "Memory is like an old dog scratching imaginary fleas anyway."

There were hundreds of people on the platform, and the train itself was filling up quickly. I knew that we had assigned seats, but still there was a sense of urgency. Not assigned seats, really, but a compartment, with whatever seats might be available. Would we sit together?

A large digital clock high on the wall above the tracks indi-cated 11:11, remarkable in itself, and yet a figure of time I'd seen so often lately that I'd begun to expect it, like the face of a stranger, someone unknown to me, who kept appearing in the most unlikely yet significant places.

I recognized many people in the crowd. They were waving at me and cheering us along.

A train loomed above the track, the dark bulk of the locomo-tive gleaming under the lights, the engine pulled up against a large triangular buttress of rubber and iron. Steam billowed from beneath the wheels and rose in clouds, disappearing into the cavernous ceiling so high above us that I could barely see the outline of the great struts holding it up.

Could this be our train? I thought. The engine is facing into the station. Is it going to back out? Is there a locomotive at the other end? I noticed the name of the train, high up on the side of the engine: El Niño. The child.

I found our compartment without any difficulty, and we did have seats together, but my wife was gone, perhaps taking care of some last-minute detail or saying goodbye to a friend. I'd already said all my goodbyes, that was a relief. Now I could look out onto the platform at all the familiar faces, some looking at me, some smiling, some without expression. I saw my two sons, and that great anguish of joy and sorrow welled up in me again, flooding my senses. But they weren't looking at me; they were thoroughly engaged in animated conversation with two young women they'd probably just met. I saw a woman standing nearby who looked at me and smiled. We both waved at the same time. I couldn't remember her name, and our connection was slipping away even as the train began to move.

My wife was sitting beside me now, resting her head on my shoulder. I took her hand as the train began to pick up speed. There were a half dozen people in the compartment. A man sitting across from me was reading a newspaper. "Where are we going?" I asked no one in particular, surprised at the sound of my own voice.

The man reading the newspaper looked up. "Italy," he said.

"Italy?" I was astonished. I couldn't believe we were going that far without a stop. I hadn't expected any of this, really, though I'd thought about it often enough.

I looked through the window and saw the platform lights slipping away, and the people under them, already leaving the station. And then we were in the tunnel, and the walls outside were black, with only an occasional small, bare light bulb in a recessed niche that passed quickly before my eyes. I looked over at my wife, her hand still in mine, her head still on my shoulder. Her eyes were closed. I looked back out the window and now all I could see in the darkness was my own reflection floating in the lights of our compartment. I couldn't see my eyes or some of the features in my face. But I recognized someone I'd known for as long as I could remember. I stared back at myself for what seemed a long time, mesmerized by the image floating in the glass.

Then I settled back in my seat against a pillow that had been thoughtfully provided for the journey, leaning my head against my wife's and closing my eyes. The train was moving faster and faster through the darkness. I felt the swaying and clicking of the car as it flew over the rails.

Matthew Polvorosa Kline, *Tule Elk at Dawn, Point Reyes National Seashore*, 2013, fine art print

Through Motions

Ariel Wish

The zipper binding my sister's bubblegum-pink raincoat laughs at me,
Wondering how long I'll fumble before she gets restless.
Her innocent belief in me leaves my heart a melted puddle,
Scaring me that one day I'll let her down.

The augmented dominant chords in Diabelli's sonatina stare me down,
Waiting for me to make one measly slip,
Shouting from underneath the shadow of black-and-white hues,
Echoing, "I told you so."

The blue-and-white porcelain that hides under stacks of mismatched bowls
        mocks me,
Predicting how long it will take me to disassemble the precarious pile,
Searching for off-balanced imperfections that result in shattered dishware,
Waiting to fail me.

The small glass buttons lining my yellow cardigan pity me,
Staring at the tips of my fumbling fingers,
Holding their breath at every lousy attempt I make.
I don't need their condolences.

Elizabeth Gorek, *Forgotten Summer*, 2016, oil on canvas, 48 × 48 inches

To Steelhead Lake

Dave Stamey

I WORKED that summer for Lee and Jennifer Roeser at McGee Creek Pack Station, on the eastern slope of the Sierra Nevada, a modest-sized outfit, maybe eighty head of stock, horses and mules combined. It was four miles of narrow winding road up the canyon before you even caught sight of the place through the willows, the last mile or so all dust and gravel and ruts, disheartening to many a tourist. Because of its remoteness, and because it was often hard to get anybody to answer the phone when you called, the dreaded day-ride business was at a minimum. Instead, we specialized in dunnage trips.

These were my favorites. Three or four mules in my string, panniers loaded with sleeping bags and tents and Coleman lanterns, and no dudes to wrangle. The owners of the stuff, Mom and Dad and the kids, would hike up with their day packs and tennis shoes, taking their time and enjoying the scenery, while I trundled up the canyon with my mules, dumped the gear off at the campsite, turned around and headed home without having to see or talk to anybody. At that point in my life I was big on not having to see or talk to people.

One morning Lee caught out three mules for me and declared that my mission for the day was to transport a bunch of duffle bags and charcoal briquettes up to a place called Steelhead Lake. I'd never been there, and I thought it was an odd thing to name a lake, since we were more than two hundred miles from the ocean and on the wrong side of the mountains to boot. The only steelhead that had ever come into this country had been filleted and packed inside some happy camper's Igloo ice chest.

Lee hunkered down and traced my route in the dirt with his finger, which is just about as much map as you're likely to get in that business. You can carry one of those topographical maps if you want, but if you try to unfold one while in the saddle your mules will spook and your horse will buck you off. The little dotted lines that are supposed to be trails are very hard to see, and anyway I've never found a topo map with the stuff on it a guy really needs, such as, "Take the fork to the right where you see that rock that looks like George Washington," or "Go on past the meadow where Gabe scared the Boy Scouts that time."

Up the canyon to Third Crossing, splash across McGee Creek and then climb a nearly vertical rock face on a set of steep and nasty switchbacks the Forest Service trail crews had been meaning to repair for the last thirty years. Top the hill and bear to the right, always to the right, and eventually I'd find it.

Lee said, "Got it?"

I nodded. You always say you've got it, even if you don't. Such is the mindset of mule packers and cowboys everywhere. Handle it? Of course I can handle it—if I couldn't handle it I wouldn't be here, by God. Then you just hope it all works out. Usually it does. This seemed simple enough. I strung up the mules, got on my horse, and rode out of the yard.

The eastern Sierra is spectacular country. It is the abrupt and soaring granite escarpment that blocks all but the fiercest storms and creates the high desert of the Great Basin. Unlike the more gradual western slope, which is well forested, the east side stands naked in its own rain shadow, and you can see the jagged peaks, the tumbled scree of the high passes, the great gray bones of the world laid bare.

Our little canyon was rugged and wind scoured as any. The trailhead stood at just over eight thousand feet, all sagebrush and manzanita, with a green belt of cottonwoods tracing the creek, and higher up the fluttering green of aspen trees. Higher still were stands of lodgepole pine, and the trails here were good, well marked and well used. This is the route everybody takes, the day hikers, the backpackers, the horsebackers. It's where geologists from all over the world come to stare at the canyon walls and point out "roof pendants," the metamorphic remains of ancient mountains that stood millions of years before the birth of the Sierra. Follow this trail all the way up and over McGee Pass, and it drops into the southern end of the Cascade Valley drainage, where you can pick up the Pacific Crest Trail—the highway of the mountains.

But turn off the main trail and wind your way through the rocks and the pumice dust and the russet carcasses of fallen trees at ten thousand feet, things begin to fade very quickly. The trails grow dim and hazy from lack of use, and in some places they are just snake tracks through the rocks—sometimes mere suggestions.

Ten or twelve miles, three or four hours at a steady slog, and eventually I found my way up there. A small, glassy lake, blisteringly blue, with pines hugging its edges and a narrow green meadow off to the left where you could find mosquitoes if you wanted any. I dumped the camp gear off at the campsite in a reasonably neat pile, sat down on a rock and ate my lunch—a peanut butter sandwich, which is really the lunch of choice for a packer. It's about the only thing you can take out of a brown paper bag after a half day in the saddle that still looks vaguely like it did when you prepared it that morning. Mayonnaise and pickle juice soaking through the white bread of a roast beef sandwich has killed the appetite of many a mountain traveler.

It was now about one o'clock in the afternoon. I sat on my rock a while longer, allowing myself to be sufficiently overwhelmed by my surroundings. I didn't go too crazy about it. Stunning alpine landscapes are wonderful things, but there was beer waiting for me at headquarters. My fellow crew members and I had a tradition of sitting on the porch as the sun went down, drinking a few, and I didn't want to miss that.

I hung the empty panniers back on the sawbucks, lashed each of them down with a neat little Gilligan hitch so they wouldn't be snagged by wayward tree branches, strung the mules up head to tail, and swung into the saddle. I was riding that day a sorrel gelding named Jasper, a common-headed guy with a swallow-forked ear and a paranoid distrust of any creature that wasn't a horse, me included. He had once carried me in a single bounding leap fifteen feet down a steep embankment and into a creek, having decided it was better to be with his friends than with me. This had happened recently enough that I was still a little miffed about it. Other than that he was a good packer's horse, and would stand dallied to the string if I had to climb off and go to adjusting things.

I yipped to the mules, swung a big circle around the camp to get them lined out, and headed for home.

And I couldn't find the damn trail.

It was a gorgeous day, temperature in the low seventies, clear skies so blue it looked like a painting, no wind to speak of—a day all gussied up to be a calendar shot. But the light had shifted into afternoon, the shadows already longer and darker on the back sides of trees and boulders, and the country I'd ridden through barely an hour before was now an entirely new world. Nothing looked the same.

I had broken one of the cardinal rules of packing: when wandering around in the mountains, always look for landmarks. You need a rock that resembles Uncle Frank's double chin, or a dead tree that reminds you of your ex-wife, something you can find again on your way back down that lets you know you're going in the right direction. I hadn't done that. I'd like to claim that I was distracted by the beauty and the grandeur, and so overcome by the sheer majesty of the mountains at ten thousand feet my brain became a-whirr with deep thoughts and philosophical musings about the insect insignificance of one man in the midst of all this granite vastness; that the spiritual joy of being where I was at that instant forced all other mundane and plebian thoughts from my head. The truth was I'd just not been paying attention.

I rode back and forth, taking horse and mules between this rock and that one, between those two trees, along a pretty steep cliff I hadn't known was there, then back to the campsite. Suddenly there were horse and mule tracks everywhere, and of course I was making more. I began to sweat a little under my hat brim. When you get a string of mules in motion, it's best to keep them in motion; as soon as you stop they get into trouble, stepping over lead ropes or wrapping each other around pine saplings, and then the wreck is on and somebody's got to jump down with a knife and start cutting things loose, and it can be hard to put it all back together. But I had to stop. I had to get my bearings back.

I sat there, looking around. I had a general sense of where I needed to go: east was over that way, and if I went far enough I could fall off the edge and tumble all the way down the canyon to the pack station, but that would be hard on equipment and livestock. What I wanted was the more elegant route.

Then I did something we all need to do more often. I gave my horse his head.

Actually, I just slacked the reins a little, while I thought stuff over. As soon as I did, Jasper shook his ears at me in disgust, as if to say, "You learned wood craft where, at Walmart?" and walked three steps to the left, found the microscopic indentation in the duff that was the trail, and we were off. That wise little fork-eared pony had spent ten summers as a packer's horse in this canyon, and of course knew every boulder and thatch of willows from the BLM campground to Big McGee Lake.

I pondered this little incident all the way back home. And for a long while after that. I'm still pondering it.

I don't mean to make more of it than it was. The drama was minimal: I hadn't been bucked off in the rocks or gotten tangled up in my lash ropes. There was no epiphany, no profound revelation. It was just something that happened, nothing more. Later, we look back and bestow on certain experiences the rank of revelation through smoky hindsight, but truth be told, the only revelation I came away with at the time was that I needed to be more observant when leading a string of mules through the wilderness. That, along with a certain hot-faced embarrassment and the hope nobody would find out about it.

What it did do was instill in me an appreciation for the endless combinations of light and geography. Landscape painters, photographers, filmmakers—I understand what they're talking about now when they speak of light and the magic it can work. I think about it when I sit on the porch at the end of the day and watch the hot yellow hills across the valley cool and soften and become inviting in the reddish shadows of the setting sun, or when I look at the slick liquid sheen on the coat of a fat bay mare in the late afternoon, or the blackness of the mountains against a pale sky in the early dawn.

Sandy White, *Roy's Redwoods*,
2004, pastel, 31 × 23 inches

All My Biographies Are Lies

Nancy Cherry

It was the year I woke late, missed mornings
out the kitchen window, missed the trail of fog,
missed the osprey, the shreds of air in his hunting wake.
But I caught the coldwater mornings of stove and sink,
days of turning around.

It was the year I promised to never regret
laundry on the basement floor, lamplight
up late, starlings in the attic, the voles,
the relentless call of night frogs.

It was a year of flood and fire. I knew
the bay had saved us, but it was too dark to see.
I accused the moon—full, gibbous, quarter, dark
or turning, but never enough. A fox drowned.
Trees exploded. Vultures spread their wings to dry.

It was a year of smoke-filled corners as rain ran up the hills.
I might say, "He did this, he did that, he forgot my name
in the night." But his heart bloomed every morning and
I missed that. He couldn't hear the bats, but he knew all
their names. Fields of wild radish understood better than I.

This morning, a breath of white through the window.
Broken bird calls. Someone's kindness alight in the trees.
Day unwinds in the open box—a ballerina turning
in her pinked room, dance of the incomplete song.
And one bird tells his story of the grocery cart
with the squeaky wheel calling up the aisles.

Jaune Evans, *Fog Heaven*, 2011, photograph

Isis Hockenos, *Side Street Chickens #1 & #2,* 2017,
India ink, gouache, colored pencil, 12 × 18 inches

Two Short Stories

Joan Thornton

SEQUENTIAL LOGIC

YES, I was there when someone robbed the bank. At the sheriff's station I am trying to remember what came before and what came after. Having little facility for recalling a sequence of events, I've devised certain methods. First, I check the placement of my markers: the great hurricane, the year of assassinations, Obama's inauguration, my high school graduation. I attempt to keep things straight so I can organize what goes between the in-between. I keep file boxes labeled places, people, headlines, happenings, sensations, shapes, and sizes, and I compulsively reorganize the files, updating, annotating, numbering, multiplying, alphabetizing, sometimes deleting the after and the before. Yes, it is confusing weaving sideways up and down. I know I was in the parking lot when the alarm sounded, but when I'm asked for an accounting my mind balks.

I'm sure my dog was barking, because we heard backfire as a car pulled away from the curb; a man clutching a laundry bag spoke into his cell phone; a woman carrying a suitcase asked a man coming out of the market for directions to the thrift store; truckers were loading boxes in back of the parking lot; a man in a grey suit rushed out of the bank swinging a briefcase. Now don't get mad, these are the facts, it's just that they might not have happened in that order.

Joan Thornton

ON THE WAY TO THE RALLY

ON THE way to the rally on my roller skates, the ones that clamp to my shoes using a key, I skate over the sidewalk in front of Unger's Variety Store. I feel a familiar chill travel up my spine. Back in '43, Ace Miller said we were rolling over spies hiding underground.

We were a gang of ten-year-old skaters, patriots all. Ace Miller, who knew about these things—he may have been eleven— said Hitler's men were holed-up in a room down there, and when we got on our knees and put our ears to the cement, we skaters agreed we heard guttural voices and the click, click, click of telegraph keys.

All these years later I'm still hearing those old spies underground, sending coded messages. They just don't seem to learn. Why, except for the cost, the blood, and the gore, no one does war their way anymore. They don't even know that they lost. I'm rolling over them on my way to the rally, skate key swinging from my neck on a string.

Giving

Stephen Ajay

we
love
dogs

because
we
can

make
them
so

happy

they
feel
the

same
about
us

Caitlin McCaffrey, *Biggie's Vision*, 2016, pigment prints

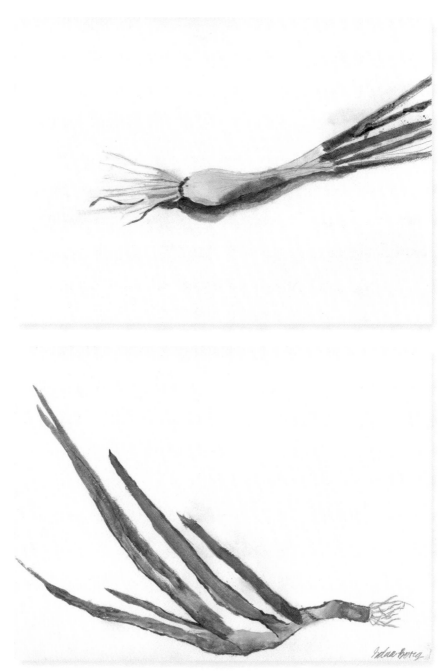

Marius Salone (above), Sofia Borg (below), Grade 7, Bolinas-Stinson School, *Young Red Onions*, 2016, watercolor, 11 × 15 inches

Spring Cleaning

Karen Benke

You box up scarves and sweaters,
boots and shoes, the years
of dusty sadness
piled on top—

With less it's easier
to relax back into yourself.
You take up hems, donate a wool dress;
keep the lace camisole, fold
turtlenecks, the frayed regret.

No more hiding—
though sometimes the old urgency
hurries back, *Come save me.*

You sing to forgive everything, reach
past the faded grief no longer in fashion.
This makes more space, a wider
opening to fill with a new find.

You slip on hat, sunglasses;
take one breath, then another—
hike a new path to the sea.

Here

Lisa Piazza

In the back yard
in the moon beam
in the night light

in the place
where what
was wasn't

I think:
everyone has
a moon memory

only mine is
seaside sick
—thick

with want
or worry.
I shrug

from safe
to sorry,
forgetting

you don't live
here anymore.
What peregrine

promise, what
fleeting form?
Mine, maybe

—gliding
footstep soft
over the

morning light:
yellow gold on the
hardwood floor.

See how
each morning
wakes like

a dream:

Cats and kids
bowls and bellies
full of milk

—happy.

Lily Andrews, Kindergarten, Bolinas-Stinson School, *Hummingbird*, 2016, marker and oil pastel on paper, 11 × 17 inches

On Religion: Oklahoma City

Barbara Heenan

1954

MY EARLIEST memories are bound in heat and drought, fanned by a forever wind blowing from the northwest across brown grasses and red clay gullies and the half-dozen scattered red-brick houses that we knew as our neighborhood. We lived in a pocket of rural neglect on the farthest outskirts of a sprawling new city that moved steadily outward, swallowing small cattle ranches, alfalfa fields, and derelict farmhouses as progress was made. On this day, far, far below the redtail spinning slow sleepy loops in a baked white sky, two tiny figures faced off. One tow headed and wide eyed, the other dark haired, lurching forward with bitten nails and clenched fists. Doreen's pond-green eyes narrowed.

"Don't you believe in the Bible?"

I felt stripped naked. Her frail legs were thin and knobby as cane poles and pale as the underbelly of fish. I didn't know how to respond. A first-grade classmate I had always disdained because of her freckles and frizzy permed hair and cheap white patent leather shoes, and whose thin dotted swiss lavender dress both fascinated and repulsed me, always making me wonder if she was perpetually chilled, and whose dad, she said, "hit hard," stood before me now. The accuser. And I stood accused, in the middle of our gravel road, frozen in confusion. The Bible, yes, old black dimpled leather, cracking and torn, always shoved to the side of the book shelf crowded out by Mother's art books.

"Don't you believe in the Lord Jesus?"

Susan Putnam, *Untitled #261*, 2016, crayon
on gessoed silk, 29 × 25 inches

Doreen's wiry brown curls quaked with righteousness. Yes, yes, Jesus I could picture. The man with the long brown hair and beard, looking up at heaven, I had been told, or yes, slashed deep in the side and bleeding, with greenish skin because he was either very sick or maybe even dead. That thought made my stomach churn. And yes, long robes too, mostly brown and not so interesting. My baby-sitter, not even a decade older than me, had taught me to sing, "Jesus loves me this I know, for the Bible tells me so." The tune was catchy and so was her enthusiasm, so I sang *con brio,* "Yes, Jesus loves me! Yes, Jesus loves me! Yes, Jesus loves me, the Bible tells me so-o-o-o!"

And once I had gone to Sunday School with her to the local Baptist Church. The teacher, not a real teacher just a lady in prim clothes, showed us paper dolls on a felt board. There were sheep and more men with long beards carrying tall curved poles, and the recognizable but undecipherable draped robes. Nothing any man I knew wore. I wasn't sure of the connection between those guys in brown blankets and Sunday, or church, or how we six or seven children in the class were supposed to behave. I didn't know what to think or do when we all knelt down to pray. So I shut my eyes at first and then peeked to see what the others were doing. The boys had a lot of hair oil shining up their scalps and hairlines. I missed my parents, and I wondered if I could go home soon. We were not allowed to touch the felt board. Only the teacher could move the cut-out figures from place to place as she told us a Bible story. How could they stick there without falling off onto the floor? And why were there no pretty princesses in dancing capes and jeweled crowns?

I was sure we didn't believe in the Bible or the Lord Jesus Christ at our house. I'd been found guilty. Doreen was right. "I think I'll go back home now," I mumbled, realizing that a friendship, if such a thing could have been possible with white patent leather shoes, had crumbled before us. How instantly it scattered away, disappearing into the dust at our feet.

✝

"Mom, why don't we go to church like everybody else?"

My question felt like one of the first rents in the close, sweet fabric of childhood. But I couldn't help asking. I had taken the step. Maybe I was missing out on something. Maybe if she could provide the answer it would soothe the heavy lump that seemed to have lodged in my chest, dogging me as I played in my room and roamed around the back yard.

"Mom?"

My mother paused, finally looked up from her ironing, taking a serious turn, exactly what I had feared. She set the hot iron up on the ironing board. Reaching over to unplug it, she nudged the basket with rolled and dampened clothes to be ironed aside with her foot. She sat down cross-legged next to it, and reached for my waist, pulling me down into her lap. My bare brown legs crossed too, nested on top of her longer brown ones, and I leaned into her. She fussed with my hair, and began the story I wanted to hear.

"We don't go to church because your dad and I don't believe in religion. In Praha when I was little we hardly ever went to church. We went every once in a while because the Czech Brethren were part of the republican movement, and we had to go because of your great grandfather and his literary causes. But Babička and Dediček preferred walks in the park and afternoon coffee on Sundays."

"What about Dad?"

"He used to go to the Catholic Church. His family was Catholic, so he went, too. He was even an altar boy in the big cathedral across the street from his Aunt Rose's house."

"What's an altar boy?"

"Altar boys help at the Mass in the Catholic Church. They help the priest and they do what he tells them to do."

"What does he tell them to do?"

"I'm not sure," she said and paused. "I think he asks them to ring bells. He asks them to carry candles and incense. And I think he asks them to hand him things when he wants them."

"Why do they do that?"

My mother looked closely into my eyes while her own smiled, and she placed her hand on my cheek.

"Barushenko, I don't really know."

"So why doesn't Dad go to church anymore?"

"It happened a long time ago. Your father made up his mind very suddenly as a very young boy to leave the church."

"How come?"

"He told me he thought it was silly—all the praying and every-one crossing themselves, and kneeling, and chanting and standing, and kneeling again. I don't think it made sense to him. One day he just got up and left the church. That's what he told me when I asked him, that's the story."

"He must have been scared."

"Yes, he must have been. It was a big step. He had to go against all the aunties who went to church a lot and wanted him to go, too. They all helped raise him and take care of him when his mother was sick and dying, so he must have felt bad going against them. But he did. One day he just decided, and he told them all he would never go back. I'm proud of him, it was a brave thing for a little boy to do."

I marked that. My father had become a crusader of sorts, a crusader for courage and independent thinking, a hero. As my mother kissed me on the top of the head and pushed me out of her lap, I held her hand. I felt better, but still I felt anxious for that small boy who had turned away and walked home alone.

Instead of church on Sundays, Dad and I often drove across the city to visit his Aunt Rose, the oldest of the sixteen aunts and uncles who had enfolded my father's boyhood. One of the uncles had been shot and killed chasing an intruder. Another had married a full-blooded Osage, beautiful Aunt Anna, who gave me an Osage-English dictionary and whose black hair flowed below her ample waist. Another became an attorney, and, of course, one was my grandfather. There were even one or two whose names my father couldn't recall because there were so many. But the oldest of the boys, Uncle John, had struck it rich in the oil fields near McAlester in the 1920s and brought the whole family up from their dirt farm near Ryan to live in Oklahoma City. Many of the brothers and sisters had lived at various times in the house on N.W. 31st Street, right across the street from the Cathedral of Our Lady of Perpetual Help, where Aunt Rose still presided. She looked after Aunt Kate, nasty and wizened and bedridden, and Aunt Lil, a divorcee and a smoker chirpy with booze, who smeared us on the cheeks with bright orange lipstick whenever we arrived.

Their house was shuttered and shaded from the sun, making it hard to see inside the warren of rooms that ran muddled toward the back screened-in porch. I made stealthy forays into the aunts' bedrooms while the adults talked, hoping to find a swatch of pink or sparkle of gold, something of light or of fantasy, but found only the darkest gloom. It was a descent into a stuffy nether world. Each aunt possessed a crucifix, with that familiar scrawny body and agonized expression, definitely dead and nailed to a cross left hanging forever on their bedroom walls. On their vanities were powder bowls with ostrich-feather puffs that smelled sweet and musty, and cracked enameled hand mirrors and hairbrushes. Only Lil's dressing table had lipsticks and nail polish and atomizers with perfume. Kate's held a phalanx of medicine bottles and a hot-water bottle. Each dressing table also held black-and-silver beads with another cross, but this time, thankfully, without the gaunt figure of Jesus. My father told me these were rosaries, as if in explanation, but I couldn't discern the roses or understand why the aunts didn't wear their beads around their necks to make them look pretty. In the deepest shadows on night stands next to each of the beds were their Bibles, black vortices pulling at my suspicion and dislike, the sight of which churned up my belly again. I never lingered long in these rooms, never found a ray of lightness. If this was the Catholic Church, then I understood my father better. He was right to leave the church and leave the aunts and their somber beliefs behind.

2016

As I opened the door of the rental car I'd parked across the street from Aunt Rose's house I felt a rush of sweet, melancholic remembrances. I hadn't been back to Oklahoma in forty years. The street was the same potholed blacktop running east and west through the once-solid neighborhood where all my father's Irish Catholic family had congregated. The block felt familiar but was now saddened, empty, and decrepit. A few cars stood in drives, lawns were bare, flowerbeds neglected, and no one walked the old-fashioned sidewalks. The house itself was still standing, though altered. The wide front window had been covered over with a Navajo-style rug to make the 1920s bungalow look more contemporary from a late-sixties hippie point of view, so I couldn't see inside the front living room as I had hoped. The front porch where Dad and I had sat in the porch swing, where Rose had served us sugary iced tea, and where we had listened to the locusts buzz, was almost bare. An abandoned charcoal grill and a pile of discarded lumber and plywood showed that someone still lived there.

Looking up and down the street, taking it in, trying to recapture it, I saw that only the Cathedral of Our Lady of Perpetual Help remained tidy and well tended. The dark-brick Renaissance-style tower cast a long, narrow shadow across the street and onto Rose's lawn, practically reaching the house itself. I was glad no one was around. I didn't want to explain what I was doing standing in a parking lot, staring at an old sad house. What did I hope to find here? I really didn't know.

Today the scars from the past—my parents' divorce, their
affairs and remarriages, my father's alcoholism and eventual suicide—
were old memories. No, not even old memories, something altogether
different, memories of memories, or even the memories of memories
of memories, still dearly held though worn derivatives of the originals.
Here now, standing in the spring sunshine on Aunt Rose's street
where I had last visited with my father, the past images were kindly.
I recalled a classic scene—a little girl walking up the front steps of this
house with her small hand in her father's larger one. As we stepped
inside the cool of the living room I saw Rose's pink cheeks and blue
eyes behind wire-rimmed spectacles, her canned spiced peaches and
pickled cucumbers lining the linoleum countertop in the kitchen, the
wobbly handshake of Aunt Kate as she fell back on her bank of bed
pillows, sighing that she was too weak to carry on, and the ebullience
of Aunt Lil as she waved her lipstick-stained cigarette around the
room, decrying the state of the world. I wondered now how Rose
could have put up with these two, the one careening toward drama
at any moment, the other determinedly seeking out the morose and
miserable. I imagine she had no choice, she was the oldest girl of
the sixteen siblings. It was Rose's duty to take care of them all. She
had been very kind to me, her sweetness like the scent of her soft,
powdery cheek still close by.

I had been on my own private pilgrimage, traveling back to
the home I had escaped so many years before, revisiting the personal
sacred sites I had created through years of reminiscing. I had driven
by my grandfather's little acreage to see if I could still find him
currying his horse or tending his chickens. All I saw was a ransacked
house and a mean pit bull chained to a stake in the front yard. And I
revisited Uncle Frank's home, where he and Aunt Euna Mae always
welcomed us with a pressed-glass bowl full of lemon drops. All there
was exactly the same. I was certain the current residents had a candy

dish on their coffee table. I drove to the house my father had pointed out to me on our Sunday drives. "That's where I grew up, honey." The same peaked roof, the same round-arched front door, and the same side porch where he and his father and mother sat in willow chairs for their family portrait, a quaint old photograph even when I was little. My pilgrimage ended here at Rose's house, the heart of things back then.

Of course, what I really wanted was to recreate them all and to hold them close to me again. I wanted to know them and understand them now that I was an adult woman, these souls that were dead but not dead within me. Especially my father. As an altar boy, dressed in a small red robe and full white, lacy collar, he was likely the pride of all the aunties. I imagined them walking across the street from their dark house to the still darker cathedral, dressed in floral prints and hats with veils, their rosaries in their hands, then sitting in the heavy wooden pews while the child who was my father assisted the priest in Sunday morning mass.

Once, he had been a cherished part of this close clan, their homes all within a radius of a mile or two of one another. What had once seemed like long distances my father and I had traveled by car to visit, these sites were, I realized after having just retraced our routes, mere minutes from one another. Their world had been so small, so contracted, with the huge cathedral looming overhead. The church had felt gloomy and ponderous to me even as a little girl and today I looked over my shoulder to observe it anew. Still there, unchanged. Then, like a slight shift in the wind before it begins to blow fully in a new direction, another story, different from the one I had held tightly to all these years, began to whisper to me.

My father, a child hero? A ten-year-old David who discovered his principles and stood against the church Goliath, the Cathedral of Our Lady of Perpetual Help, dominating this small family, this small house, this small boy?

I recollected a photograph I had of my father, framed and hanging on my study wall where I saw it several times a day. It was taken around 1930, when he must have been ten or eleven, perhaps even as old as twelve. His face is petal soft, with full sweet lips and big luminous eyes. His hair is stylishly cut and carefully combed to show his broad forehead. He is a very pretty boy. The photo shows the first, freshest bloom of the handsome man he became. But there is something very sad in this photo that has always drawn me to it, like a crepuscular bird call reflecting the pulling away of the day. I saw the picture of him again in front of me. And I see now that he is trying to hide. Even though he is sitting dutifully for this portrait in his best coat and tie, he is hiding from the camera, drawing away. He is not just shy or retiring, as I had always interpreted the story this strange, ambivalent photo had to tell. Now I saw clearly the shame in the duck of his chin and in the dark deep pool of his eyes. I hear what he is saying silently. For the first time.

Amanda Tomlin, *Laird's Boathouse*, 2016, salted paper ziatype

Henry Evans Poppies

Barry Roth

Seen so exactly the flags
of the *copa de oro* no longer confuse.
The style, fulfilled,
moves upward with precision
—one might almost say
           acceptance,
except to do so would be
to heap confusion on the scene.

Left alone the petals
will begin to radiate light
and seem larger, brighter than
mere calipers would report
and clarity is out the door.

But by then, as in romance,
you will not wish to count
the gray-green filaments
of leaves.
           Too much exactitude
would read like
failure, separation, loss.

Jani Gillette, *You Wearing You*, 2015, pen and ink on paper, 11 × 14 inches

Christel Dillbohner, *Iridescent Cloud*, 2014, oil on wood, 30 × 30 inches

Prepare for Landing

G. David Miller

BACK IN the eighties, my work took me quite often to West Africa. If it were Ghana or Nigeria, the connecting flights back to the States went through London Heathrow. If Senegal, Côte d'Ivoire, and other nations tied to Le Metropole, it was Paris Charles de Gaulle.

One morning, sitting in the waiting lounge at the gate to catch my TWA flight from Paris to Washington Dulles, I noticed an elderly man dressed in a *dishdasha*, the white Saudi robe we often see in photos. What caught my attention was that he was wearing rubber flip-flops and carrying a soiled cloth bag. I could not but notice that he was bareheaded and his robe was threadbare. I recall thinking that this was not the typical Saudi businessman flying first class to Washington to close an important deal.

He appeared a bit disoriented as he tried to find a place to sit in the crowded lounge. Instinctively, I hopped up and, taking his arm, led him to a seat nearby. I then forgot about him as I became engrossed in my complimentary copy of *Le Monde*.

I do not recall seeing him board, nor did I think about him during the long flight. Then, perhaps an hour from landing, I was wakened from a nap induced by a double Scotch by some shouting from the back of the plane.

"I want to see your passport," the female flight attendant was shouting. "I need to see your I-90."

I and everyone else turned and looked down the aisle toward this poor man in his *dishdasha*, sitting alone among three empty seats. He looked utterly confused. The flight attendant was towering over him and, with one look, she managed to convey the discountenance of the functionary whose directions were not being obeyed, let alone understood. The solution in such situations is to yell louder.

We all watched in silence. In that one hour before landing, there was no other distraction available, the meal having been served, the film completed, and the screen rolled up. After a couple more attempts, the stewardess turned and looked up and down the aisle.

By now I had begun to feel that this man was my responsibility. I had lived long enough in the Middle East to feel that he was someone I could relate to, perhaps someone jammed next to me in a taxi or selling me something in the *suq*. He was someone's grandfather, sitting on a bus on his way into town to do his shopping.

The Arabic at my disposal was of a local Maghrebian dialect that could buy me a chicken and some vegetables at the market in Fez but could not promise me much in the Gulf. Nevertheless, I figured Why not? I'll give it a try.

I offered my assistance. The stewardess readily accepted and walked away. I gestured silently at the empty aisle seat; the old man squinted at me for a moment and then nodded. I sat down.

He watched me intently as I settled in. I greeted him in Arabic. He greeted me back. We then sat in further silence listening to the roar of the engines. I asked him if this was his first visit to America. He said that this was his first time on a plane. He had never left Saudi Arabia before. Then we sat in silence again.

After putting the words together in my head, I told him that a paper was to be completed before we landed and I would help him if he would give me his passport. Reaching down for his cloth bag, he pulled out his crisp new passport and we began the task. I asked him for the details: What was the purpose of his visit? Where did he plan to stay, and for how long? He shrugged and said he didn't know.

I asked again, making sure that my voice did not increase in decibels. "Why did you come to America?" I tried to ask in as disinterested yet friendly a manner as possible.

He pointed at his face and said, "My eyes."

I focused on his eyes for the first time and clearly saw he had cataracts. "Are you going to a doctor in the States?" I asked.

"*Inshallah,*" he answered. May it be God's will. We fell into silence again.

"Do you have the name of a doctor?"

"*'Allah yuaffir,*" he said. God provides. This is the same response one gives when approached by a beggar in the street, as if I was begging him for the name of his doctor and he was reluctant to give it. Then I realized that, in fact, he really did not know where he was going. I was surprised by the insouciance of someone traveling far from home for the first time, armed with no other language, no idea where he was headed, and handicapped by poor vision.

I could feel that my Arabic was running out. With one final try, I mustered up enough words to ask if anyone would be there to meet him or if he knew where he was going when he got off the plane. His answer once more was "*'Allah yuaffir.*"

By then I began to wonder whether he was actually clueless, or was he playing with me? I did not know what to do for my new friend.

I went back to my seat for the final few minutes of our flight. The flight attendant brought me a half bottle of Champagne in gratitude. She smiled and thanked me. I said, "Can you have the pilot radio the tower at Dulles?"

Did she look nervous, or did I imagine it? "Sure," she said tentatively.

"This man seems not to have any idea where he is going when he gets off the plane, and I'm concerned about him. When I ask if there will be anyone to meet him, all he says is that God provides."

She seemed to understand and said she would ask TWA's ground crew to call the Saudi embassy in D.C. to advise them that a citizen of theirs appears to be confused and soon will be wandering about aimlessly in Virginia in a *dishdasha* and flip-flops.

I gulped down the Champagne and followed instructions to prepare for landing, once again forgetting the old man in the back.

When the plane landed, I went through the usual drill of grabbing my roller board from above and impatiently waiting to get off and get in line for passport control. I had, at the time, a black diplomatic passport. However, this only made life more complicated for me. I am certain that Dulles is the only airport where the line for the U.S. diplomatic passport is longer than the regular line.

There I was, craning my head to see how much longer I had before hopping a cab home after an interminable three weeks away, when I felt a tug at my sleeve.

There he was, about to pass by me, flanked by two Saudis in matching dark suits, obviously from the embassy. He recognized me in spite of his poor eyes. He stopped for just a quick second and, cracking a broad smile, said in English, "God provides."

Philip Bone, *Three Masks*, 2011, mixed media on canvas, 26 × 33 inches

Monk's Empty Eye
Thomas Hickey

Meanwhile, let us have a sip of tea.
Milkweed settles over the river.
The blue heron crosses the bank.

An old friend sings of the moon
and stars by the fire that warms
our feet. Her voice is windblown,

impartial. Lonely lovers will call
us home, away from cool currents
and fish huddled in oak root beds.

The owl rises in its nest, coos.
Darkness spreads through the trees.
I try to look at the fire

with a monk's empty eye,
but there's a long way to wander
and so much I might need. For now I watch

the waking owl, and laugh with my friends
at the beautiful foolishness of things.

May Ta, *Somber Summer*, 2016,
mixed media, 10 × 8 inches

Toni Littlejohn, *Fire Under Ice*, 2015, latex enamel, acrylics, tempera paint on canvas, 48 × 72 inches

The Blows

Kaitlyn Gallagher

for Rachael Zucker

NATURE IS brutal.

In the leafy shadows of any forest, death abounds. Oceans and deserts, plains and mountains, swamps and fields; in the skies and beneath the ground, animals kill and die, thousands every savage second. Blood soaks the earth in such quantities, the very grass under our feet should grow red.

But humans, thumb-proud bipedals, eschew these horrors. We like our nature sanitized—we choose nature that soothes, nature that elevates our senses and sparkles with a suggestion of the divine, or is just refreshingly pretty and quaint.

Enter our ducks.

First there were four, and their lives were fine. They quacked, ate, and splashed around in the pond. One died a clean, inexplicable death, and the other three lived to become old ladies. Farmyard paranoids, they often burst out with loud, long rounds of quacking apropos of nothing, then went suddenly silent, as if waiting for a response, or the apocalypse. They met our human needs: they were cute, quaint, comic—laying their waxy blue ova any-old-where in the yard, like an afterthought.

As small-time, front-yard farmers, we are leapers, not lookers. On a trip to the feed store one day, we noticed a large enclosure of wee ducklings. No animal reaches the Platonic ideal of *adorable* as a baby duck does (even when they are sheltering in your bathroom and making a mighty stench), so we gathered five of different breeds and carried them home. Because they were too delicate to live outdoors when small, we started the ducklings in a giant plastic tub made cozy with wood shavings, water trough, and feeder beneath a heat lamp. Their intense cuteness comes from their looks—the tiny perfect bills, their translucent eyelids that close slowly when they doze off in your hand, the unlikely, electric orange of their webbed feet. Some also seem to be smiling slyly out of the corners of their bills, in a way that a human might, but a dog never would.

You can't sex ducks young, meaning that the male and female ducks aren't distinguishable from each other until their adolescence. Too late, in other words, to be able to leave the boys behind.

It's not their fault. Male ducks will be male ducks, and it soon became clear that we had a few in our new brood. Their pubescent quacks were a kind of parched croak, and although all ducklings grow at a startling rate, the males grew even faster. But the biggest indicator that we had boys in the mix was their aggression. With necks outstretched, they darted at the others. At first these attacks were haphazard and seemed half-hearted, but once the young ones graduated to the farmyard, the brutality of their behaviors came of age.

Around this time I learned I had cancer.

A handful of ducklings might result in some males. Statistically likely. My family history of cancer made my cancer statistically likely. But as with the baby ducks, whose exquisite cuteness I enjoyed every moment of without worrying whether there were males among them, I never dwelled on the likelihood that I, too, would develop cancer. I savored my pre-cancer existence.

Cancer was written in me for a long time, scrawled on the wall inside my head. All that had been added was a period to replace the question mark.

But I was afraid to die, and I spent some weeks on the outside of life, dissociated from the world because inside I had cancer, and only I had it, while outside people were choosing pastries and waiting at stop signs and walking their dogs. Surreal.

That outsideness quickly forced me inside, deeper into experience than I had allowed myself before for fear of feeling too much. Now I felt everything, urgently. Touching my daughters' skin, their hair, holding my husband's hand, sitting in the sunshine on a cold day, all hit me potently with the suggestion of their loss.

When you have cancer, they will cut it out if they can. If they can cut it out, that's good. It doesn't seem good, but it is. None of it seems good, and you will find yourself thinking, *What if I just run, what if I stand up off of this examining table and leaving everything and everyone behind me, walk out, blue robe hanging open at my naked back, past my smart and kind and likeable surgeon, past my terrified and loving husband, down the hallway, looking only for the exit sign, past the patients waiting in the waiting room where the décor suggests nothing of the dreadful nature of the real business at hand, past the helpful receptionist with the sweet sense of humor, past the ancients waiting in the lobby and standing impatient, confused, and in pain at the pharmacy, through the sliding door and out under the sky, which is real, through the parking lot full of cars that will never have cancer, up the hill and out into the dirt and scrub grasses, further up to where the real trees start and people aren't, where the air gets colder and greener and darker, up further, legs aching, skin chilled, deep in the nowhere of the hills, unfindable, unhelpable, untreatable, unpitiable, unadmirable, unknown, off the appointment list, off the surgery schedule, off the lab slides, samples unstudied, genes untested, cancer unfound, body intact?*

The term for my surgery—bilateral mastectomy—is vaguely nautical and geometric, as if a two-masted schooner were being decommissioned by a math teacher. But I don't blame medicine for its obfuscation—honest descriptors make anxious patients. I knew it would be wretched and I was willing. I knew it would be preceded by fear and followed by pain both intense in the short term and persistent in the long term. Following the surgery, I knew there might be poisonous treatments, pills and potions and IVs killingly potent, and I was willing. I was willing to do it all, for the touch of my daughters' hair, my husband's hand, the weak sunlight on a cold day.

Around this time my husband came to me with a proposal. He asked if I had seen the young drakes' behavior—how mean and even brutal they were to the older female ducks. Mounting their backs, the drakes held the females' heads underwater by gripping their necks with their sharp bills. The females thrashed and struggled not to drown, but could not get away until the drakes released them.

His proposal? Harvest the males. "Harvest" is farm-talk for slaughter. For kill.

The prospect of my surgery ahead of me, I didn't want any blood, any cries of pain, any death to come close. I needed life, and in its gentlest forms, surrounding me just then.

But then I witnessed it. As I sat reading in the yard our old white duck, Lady Jane, waddled past. Our old ducks are Indian Runners, a breed with a long, elegant neck held high. Running down the back of Lady Jane's neck was a bloody, open wound, dirty and deep. Later I saw one of the male ducks hold another female down in the dirt, ripping the feathers from her neck as she struggled and cried out.

In the wild, these ducks would have thousands of miles of air and land in which to coexist or escape each other. Here, in an arena of our making, we allowed this bloodshed by disallowing their escape. It's possible that the males' aggression was even intensified by their confinement in our yard—perhaps in the wide world they would have enough space to feel secure without these frequent displays of dominance.

Or not. Nature is brutal. Perhaps we were just seeing up close what from a distance is invisible—the pain of existence as an animal.

I was away from the farm on harvest day. One of my daughters, a farmer at heart, assisted her dad with enthusiasm. My younger daughter and I spent a luxurious, death-free afternoon at a bookstore, browsing and perusing, lunching and talking.

The fine-feathered bullies, whose plumage was as gorgeous as their behavior was ugly, were quickly and cleanly transitioned into harmless future suppers. Their appearance on the dinner table is as yet unscheduled, but I will not partake, knowing them as I did when their small fluffy bodies, warm in my palm, relaxed into sleep, sly smiles on their little beaks.

Cancer is nature. It is growth. It is growth that ends in death, as is all life. We arrest it as best we can, treasuring life. But it is also a part of life, life in a fearsome form, in a form that might end our own. My own.

It's not personal. Like the drakes' treatment of the females, the nature of their organism drove their actions; the nature of my cells drove them toward malignancy. Did I cause it? No. Could I have prevented it? No. Does it inform my identity? No. The changes to my body and the threat of mortality are personal, but the cancer is not.

After we killed the ducks, we discovered two roosters among our chickens. Two more dinners in the freezer. Where does it end? Can we attempt to curb the brutality of the world, knowing we will never succeed? Knowing that once we turn our hand to rescue a bug from a puddle, behind our back a bird falls from its nest?

It does not end. So I must accept brutality, loss, separation, suffering, meanwhile taking what action I can to lessen it, temper it, soften the blows landing all around me.

Oh, Animals

Satchel Trivelpiece

How I want to
and wonder how to
turn into you
for a day
and see what you
have to say.

When the dog barks
and a bird chirps
are they saying something?

Oh, how I wish to talk to you.
I'm a little troubled.
Why can't I talk to you,
when we say we are animals?

So I guess we all have our own languages
and here is a question for you:
Does the tiger understand the bird?
And when the bird
is being hunted by the tiger,
does the bird have a singing chirp
or a mercy chirp?
And when the bird
is being hunted by the tiger,
does the bird have anything to say,
or was the bird just waiting for this moment?

Xander Weaver-Scull, *Arctic Peregrine Falcons: An Endangered Species Now Recovered*, 2015, monoprint, hand-drawn and hand-cut acetate stencils with homemade earth paints (from Lagunitas and Sierra foothills) on Stonehenge paper, 24 × 30 inches

Bolinas.
February 23rd.

My dear Duchess -

Of course you recognise the place. It is just as fine as ever - but dearie me! - the weather - it is fierce - the wind is blowing terrifically and the rain is coming down in sheets & blankets - the bed & the whole thing - It is not one storm we have had but many - When we first came out the weather was delicious. - such perfect sunshine - eeescholtzias a bloomin' - & the grass a growin' - I will try to express in my next letter just how we and the storm appeared to the world of Bolinas - just between us 3 I think Ma is getting a wee bit tired of all the down pour. She told me this morning she thought she would go in about the "12th" to gather in all her birthday presents - And't you missing dear old Mackie - the darling little sinner. Why doth you look so "Root" - He spends most of his time in the cellar. We are afraid he will not his little tootsies

I thought you might like to have a view of us as we left Kents. Can you see your "highness" standing at the front door bidding us adieu. I hope you know "who is who". Ash says she never came down on such a jog trot.

I wish you could have seen the little station where we had filled it all up with our luggage there was scarce room ~~to~~ enough to get to the ticket office and purchase our tickets — that may seem like an exaggeration to you — Mother clung to her beloved Jerusalem cherry for dear life — we all had our special pets to look out for. You can well imagine mine was Maci-doodles the wicked old sinner.

just to let you see
I have not exaggerated
I have attempted to
picture just the way
we & our "pets" & all
our belongings looked
ere we departed
on the train — I
felt sorry for that
poor ticket agent
he even had to
put Mac in the
baggage car — I am
sure he is now on
the rest cure — somewhere —

OVERLEAF AND ABOVE Letters from Grace Nichols and Belle Nichols Southworth to their mother, Ellen Wolcott Foster Nichols, with watercolor illustrations depicting life in Bolinas, California, circa 1902. Courtesy of the Tully family

What It Takes

Cynthia Fontaine Reehl

> *levitation*
> *the paraplegic*
> *the rhinoceros*
> *the man with the frog*
> *the question*
> *the tornado*
> *the rhinoceros again*
> *the answer*

FIRST YOU'LL have to get there. Around your house, through the rose garden, around the world, to your desk. You'll switch on your computer and look outside. It's summer. The treetops, thick and swishing in the August sky, will call to you. Good. Because that's where you'll have to go. Straight up. Will yourself out the window and into the sky. Suspend yourself with the bravado of an explorer.

Once you've accepted that you are somehow weightless, that your feet can no longer touch the ground, characters will come. You'll meet a paraplegic who looks like John Turturro. His teeth will be black and, without speaking, he'll kiss you, pressing you to the floorboards in a winter room with no heat. He'll invite you for cocktails at the Counterpoint Café and you'll accept. While you're there, his fetish friends with their whip tails and executioner's masks will break into your house and steal your silver.

You'll see a rhinoceros trotting through October woods. There will be a stone castle, each stone a carved rose, and two white ponies with manes the electric colors of tropical fish. You'll remember a day decades ago, riding your bike through falling leaves, ruby leaves, the sky dazzling and a fox in the meadow.... At the top of

Prospect Hill, you stood up on your pedals, let go of the handlebars and flew. You'll remember. A voice will suddenly boom through the woods like a public address. It's the rhinoceros. Here's what he'll tell you: "There are two sisters. One of them has vowed to never tell the truth. Don't kill her."

A man will emerge from the blue-green hills of Tennessee. He'll lift his face to the sun and sigh. He'll notice a frog, then cup his hands into a murky pond and drink an extraordinary amount of water.

You'll have to ask these characters a thing or two. Like, "What do you want?" Make them tell you the first thing that comes to their minds. Nothing big. What does the wind want, tearing through the streets, pitching bats through the gables? "What do you want?" Nothing big. Just ask. Ask. Ask again.

The man from Tennessee, his motivation will be clear. He wants clean water for his planet. He wants simply what the frog has—a frog pond. And to quench his thirst. Water will solve it. Why, water, way.

This is the way. You'll find that it gets easier. Maybe you'll be ready for the day the sky will swirl black with doom, sending people skittering for safety, sending churches spinning like UFOs into outer space. When this tornado hits, you'll know for sure that it has come for you. Maybe you'll walk toward it, attracted, willing. There will be moments when you'll think you're going to die and no one will ever know how or why or when. No good-byes, no loved ones, just you alone: a naked woman wearing emerald earrings, straddling a cyclone. Maybe you won't stop.

If you're willing, if you go, you'll go somewhere no one else can get to. And your feet will touch the ground.

You'll be back. Eventually, the rhinoceros will reappear. He'll ask, "What's the answer?"

And you'll have to have one.

Waste in Paradise

Chalk Drawings on Found Objects by Julia Edith Rigby

TUNDRA ART

Bear Flood II

TWO SUMMERS AGO, in 2015, I packed some sketchbooks and trekked through Iceland and Greenland, ultimately arriving in Kulusuk, a small village in east Greenland. I'd arrived at a time of transition—seasonal, global, and cultural. Summer's cotton grass blooms were giving way to autumn's northern lights, local hunters were flensing seals on the beach, the Greenland ice sheet was melting at an alarming rate.

Searching to understand what made the tundra so impossibly beautiful, I found fox tracks, belly flowers, and a midnight sun. I also found plastic crammed into rocky crevices, Styrofoam bobbing on the incoming tide, and oil drums rusting on snow fields.

Texaco Seals I

After spending time among these oil drums, I decided to make them my canvases. At the time, I was painting a mural in a local school to celebrate Sassuma Arnaa, Goddess of the Sea. I was intrigued with the children's tale of how the goddess suffers from trash and pollution—a modern addition to the ancient stories.

I hauled the beached oil drums atop icebergs and chalked them with images of wild creatures. I collaborated with the rising tide, documenting the ways the water swallowed oil drums and erased my images of walruses, polar bears, and seals.

The resulting work represents my efforts to understand this beautiful land, and to reckon with the forces that trouble it.

Melting Walrus I

Songbird on the Tundra

Dead Reckoning

David Swain

Moss underfoot, we imagine the salmon
In her cold river realm, gape-jawed, juddering,
Hovering above ochre cobbles,
Her tail a shredded pennant in the steadfast current.
Ferns arch tenderly above her redd,
Tips to the riffles, forming bower and bier.

Fresh to salt, salt to fresh, the flesh hued a faint maroon
A vessel etched with fate-flecked alchemy
Navigating by lodestar and molecular reacquaintance
Returning to the natal bend in a brook
Her homecoming her undoing.

She musters one last feint, fans away silt and tails' remains,
Senses her moment. Her quivering mate looms alongside,
The water roils with roe and milt,
A small galaxy forms and cools. Stars descend.
She is spent. Scales fall from her like small dimes,
Coruscant on the gravel.

We do not think of her at night.
Each dark rill buffeting her torpid form,
Bobbing gently. A kingfisher's blue blurts from a laurel,
Cackling benediction and elegy.
And the dam hulks above, concrete seething in slow, slow dissolve.

Van Waring, *Coastal Cross Section*, 2015, pen and ink, watercolor, 8 × 12 inches

Rich Clarke, *Kehoe Morning*, 2006, photograph

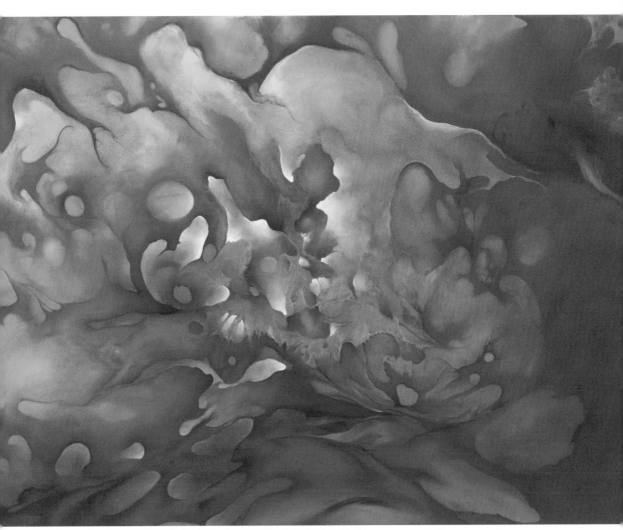

Johanna Baruch, *Enthymesis*, 2013, oil on panel, 36 × 48 inches

DANCING

Robert Hass

The radio clicks on—it's poor swollen America,
up already and busy selling the exhausting obligation
of happiness while intermittently debating whether or not
a man who kills 50 people in five minutes
with an automatic weapon he has bought for the purpose
is mentally ill. Or a terrorist. Or if terrorists
are mentally ill. Because if killing large numbers of people
with sophisticated weapons is a sign of sickness—
you might want to begin with fire, our early ancestors
drawn to the warmth of it—from lightning,
must have been, the great booming flashes of it
from the sky, the tree shriveled and sizzling,
must have been, an awful power, the odor
of ozone a god's breath; or grass fires,
the wind whipping them, the animals stampeding,
furious, driving hard on their haunches from the terror
of it, so that to fashion some campfire of burning wood,
old logs, must have felt like feeding on the crumbs
of the god's power and they would tell the story
of Prometheus the thief, and the eagle that feasted
on his liver, told it around a campfire, must have been,
and then—centuries, millennia—some tribe
of meticulous gatherers, some medicine woman,
or craftsman of metal discovered some sands that,
tossed into the fire, burned blue or flared green,
so simple the children could do it, must have been,

or some soft stone rubbed to a powder that tossed
into the fire gave off a white phosphorescent glow.
The word for *chemistry* from a Greek—some say Arabic—
stem associated with metal work. But it was in China
2,000 years ago that fireworks were invented—
fire and mineral in a confined space to produce power—
they knew already about the power of fire and water
and the power of steam: 100 BC, Julius Caesar's day.
In Alexandria, a Greek mathematician produced
a steam-powered turbine engine. Contain, explode.
"The earliest depiction of a gunpowder weapon
is the illustration of a fire-lance on a mid-12th century
silk banner from Dunhuang." Silk and the Silk Road.
First Arab guns in the early 14th century. The English
used cannons and a siege gun at Calais in 1346.
Cerigna, 1503: the first battle won by the power of rifles
when Spanish "arquebusters" cut down Swiss pikemen
and French cavalry in a battle in southern Italy.
(Explosions of blood and smoke, lead balls tearing open
the flesh of horses and young men, peasants mostly,
farm boys recruited to the armies of their feudal overlords.)
How did guns come to North America? 2014,
a headline: DIVERS DISCOVER THE SANTA MARIA.
One of the ship's Lombard cannons may have been stolen
by salvage pirates off the Haitian reef where it had sunk.
And Cortes took Mexico with 600 men, 17 horses, 12 cannons.
And LaSalle, 1679, constructed a seven-cannon barque,
Le Griffon, and fired his cannons upon first entering the continent's

interior. The sky darkened by the terror of the birds.
In the dream time, they are still rising, swarming,
darkening the sky, the chorus of their cries sharpening
as the echo of that first astounding explosion shimmers
on the waters, the crew blinking at the wind of their wings.
Springfield Arsenal, 1777. Rock Island Arsenal, 1862.
The original Henry rifle: a 16-shot .44 caliber rimfire
lever-action, breech-loading rifle patented—it was an age
of tinkerers—by one Benjamin Tyler Henry in 1860,
just in time for the Civil War. Confederate casualties
in battle: about 95,000. Union casualties in battle:
about 110,000. Contain, explode. They were throwing
sand into the fire, a blue flare, an incandescent green.
The Maxim machine gun, 1914, 400–600 small-caliber rounds
per minute. The deaths in combat, all sides, 1914–1918
was 8,042,189. Someone was counting. Must have been.
They could send things whistling into the air by boiling water.
The children around the fire must have shrieked with delight.
1920: Iraq, the peoples of that place were "restive"
under British rule and the young Winston Churchill
invented the new policy of "aerial policing" which amounted,
sources say, to bombing civilians and then pacifying them
with ground troops. Which led to the tactic of terrorizing civilian
populations in World War II. Total casualties in that war,
worldwide: soldiers, 21 million; civilians, 27 million.
They were throwing sand into the fire. The ancestor who stole
lightning from the sky had his guts eaten by an eagle.
Spreadeagled on a rock, the great bird feasting.

They are wondering if he is a terrorist or mentally ill.
London, Dresden. Berlin. Hiroshima, Nagasaki.
The casualties difficult to estimate. Hiroshima:
66,000 dead, 70,000 injured. In a minute. Nagasaki:
39,000 dead, 25,000 injured. There were more people killed,
100,000, in more terrifying fashion in the firebombing
of Tokyo. Two arms races after the ashes settled.
The other industrial countries couldn't get there
fast enough. Contain, burn. One scramble was
for the rocket that delivers the explosion that burns humans
by the tens of thousands and poisons the earth in the process.
They were wondering if the terrorist was crazy. If he was
a terrorist, maybe he was just unhappy. The other
challenge afterwards was how to construct machine guns
a man or a boy could carry: lightweight, compact, easy to assemble.
First a Russian sergeant, a Kalashnikov, clever with guns
built one on a German model. Now the heavy machine gun,
the weapon of European imperialism through which
a few men trained in gunnery could slaughter native armies
in Africa and India and the mountains of Afghanistan,
became "a portable weapon a child can operate."
The equalizer. So the undergunned Vietnamese insurgents
fought off the greatest army in the world. So the Afghans
fought off the Soviet army using Kalashnikovs the CIA
provided to them. They were throwing powders in the fire
and dancing. Children's armies in Africa toting AK-47s
that fire 30 rounds a minute. A round is a bullet.
An estimated 500 million firearms on the earth.

One hundred million of them are Kalashnikov-style semi-automatics.
They were dancing in Orlando, in a club. Spring night.
Gay Pride. The relation of the total casualties to the history
of the weapon that sent exploded metal into their bodies—
30 rounds a minute, or 40, is a beautifully made instrument,
and in America you can buy it anywhere—and into the history
of the shaming culture that produced the idea of Gay Pride—
they were mostly young men, they were dancing in a club,
a spring night. The radio clicks on. Green fire. Blue fire.
The immense flocks of terrified birds still rising
in wave after wave above the waters in the dream time.
Crying out sharply as the French ship breasted the vast interior
of the new land. America. A radio clicks on. The Arabs,
a commentator is saying, require a heavy hand. Dancing.

For the story of the Kalashnikov, see C. J. Chivers,
The Gun, *New York: Simon & Schuster, 2011.*

Lili Marlene

Michel Venghiattis

Taken in Paris in August, 1944, a few days before the Allies marched in. The fellows in
civilian clothes are all Resistance fighters, with sympathetic gendarmes in attendance.
My father, Alexis, on the right, is holding up a rifle. I assume they are standing
in front of a government building that was liberated from the Nazis.

MY PARENTS WERE decorated heroes in the French Resistance.
They each received commemorative plaques signed by General
Eisenhower for their service in harboring and nursing a badly
burned American pilot in their farmhouse in Normandy until
he was well enough to make his way to Spain.

Several months before the Resistance liberated Paris ahead of
the advancing Allies, my father made a delivery of gunpowder
to a Resistance hideout there, transporting it on the back of a
converted bicycle mini-flatbed. It was the middle of the night,

My family in 1943, before I was born, with the cart they pulled
from Normandy all the way to Paris after neighbors informed on
them to the Gestapo. Whenever they heard a plane flying overhead,
everyone jumped into the bushes for fear of getting strafed.

———

well past the Nazi curfew. This was very risky in itself, as the
Nazis routinely imprisoned people they picked up after cur-
few. Whenever a Nazi soldier was killed by the Resistance, the
Nazis would send ten prisoners to the firing squad.

A true family story: My father is wheeling his cart full of gunpowder down a dark narrow street when he sees a Nazi patrol
heading in his direction. Not knowing what to do, he starts
whistling "Lili Marlene," the Nazi hit tune of the Occupation.
The patrol give him big smiles as they cross paths, and he
wheels his load of gunpowder to its destination.

A Bowl's Circumference

Deborah Buchanan

These cracked, parched hands
dig into the earth,
burrowing into flecked fragments
of glacier, mountain, and riverbed,
searching through coarse darkness,
releasing the scent of other lives:
the furry brown mole's twitching star nose
set quivering by endless pathways of desire;
or the single white root,
stretching down
through history
to the hidden rivers
of sediment,
and the wet clay yields
to the knowledge
of how a pot, a curve
of burnished black
etched with pale geometries,
will become hard and useful,
sitting on a shelf
full of grain or water,
or an endless emptiness
where worlds are formed
in the chapped lines
of patience and persistence.

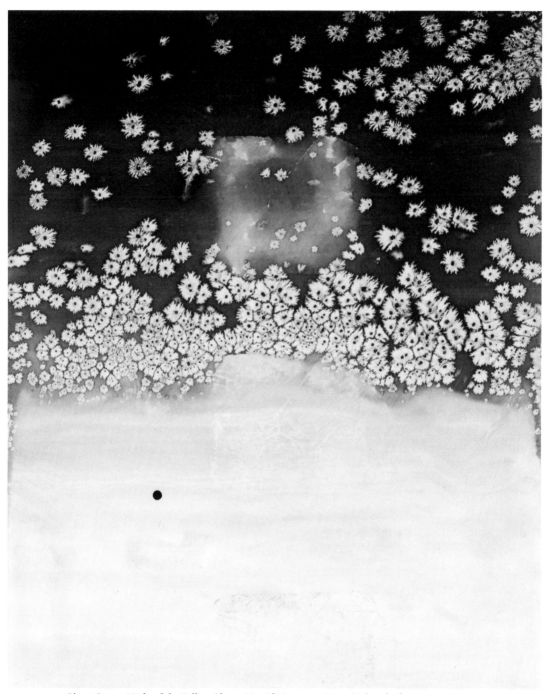

Glenn Carter, *Night of the Falling Flower/Lucid N13-2*, 2016, sumi ink and salt on gesso paper, 18 × 12 inches. Collection: Crocker Art Museum, Sacramento, California

Sherrie Lovler, *Crossroads*, 2016, sumi ink, acrylic ink, gold leaf, gouache, 8 × 8 inches

Emergency Lock-Down Drill
Prartho Sereno

Yesterday the third graders and I were writing about clouds
when it was announced that the Emergency Lock-Down Drill
was about to begin, during which we were to run and hide,
to find a place—behind the teacher's desk or under the oversized
cushions in the reading corner—where we could disappear.
Then the three shrill bursts, and the teacher raced to lock the door,
pull the blinds, douse the lights, all the while reminding us—
this teacher with a plum-blossom face, voice of a faraway cloud—
she told us to, please, stay still as stones, as if nobody were here.
And, as best we could, we did. Me, crouched next to the sink,
under the paper towel dispenser, the principal's commander-in-chief
voice oozing in through the PA. If someone dangerous were
running through the halls, he said, he should not be able
to see you. And so we sank deeper into the thickening dark,
trying to be small, but leaking out all over, at the edges of things.

Mary Siedman, *Bolinas Beach*, 2016, oil on panel, 14 × 18 inches

Next Time

Molly Giles

HER FATHER hadn't said a word since Waterloo, and Ginny, behind the wheel of the rented Renault, couldn't tell if he was asleep or angry, though why would he be angry? He had fussed about in the Wellington Museum for hours this morning and had spent this entire afternoon stumping around the rundown Dunkirk seawall with an old military map in his hand while she trailed behind, pretending to be interested. He was doing exactly what he'd always wanted to do, touring the battlefields and war sites he had read about for years, and if she wished they were seeing more art museums and wandering through more outdoor markets, well, she could always come back to Europe later, couldn't she, on her own, after Papa was gone? She glanced over at him sitting erect in the passenger seat beside her, his brown collar pulled up, his brown cap pulled down, his sunglasses propped on his large nose, his swollen hands folded on the crook of his cane. He was almost ninety and would not last forever. "I love you, old terror," she said, knowing his hearing aid was turned off. Then she turned back to the road ahead of her.

Normandy looked as deceptively peaceful under the warm June sun as Belgium had. Fields of wheat and short green corn stretched on either side of the highway, interspersed with the black-hearted scarlet poppies they had seen everywhere. *In Flanders fields the poppies blow/between the crosses, row on row…* she had the rest written down in her journal to share with her middle-school students in the fall. She knew her father was seeing this placid countryside as the war zone it had been in the 1940s, all torn up, mud and barbed wire everywhere, helicopters landing and taking off, cots filled with the wounded and dying, but it made her too sad to think of it that way. The slaughter of all those boys? A waste.

"It had to be done," her father had stated calmly over dinner last night, and Ginny knew better than to argue. Anyway, her argument would have been specious, for she had been thinking only of herself. One of those boys sacrificed in The Invasion, she'd been thinking, might have gone on to have a son and that son might have grown up to be the man for her, Virginia Jane Harris. If only her intended father-in-law had not been shot down in 1944, she reasoned, she might be sitting across from her soul mate right now instead of counting out pills for a cranky old man who still treated her as if she were fifteen. "It's bad Darwin," she decided.

Her father had looked pointedly at the wine glass in her hand. "*Hitler* was bad Darwin," he'd said. This trip was hard on him, too. Ginny had not been his first choice of companion. But he'd outlived everyone else: he'd been widowed twice, and his friends in the Rotary Club were dropping like flies. He was stuck with her, his only child. And it wasn't so bad. They were having fun. In a grim sort of way.

She eased the car now through the narrow main street of a postcard-pretty village lined with stone and half-timbered houses that looked as if they had stood there, untouched, for centuries, and glanced at the address she had written down. Her father was paying for this trip, but he was a frugal man, and Ginny had not always been able to find inexpensive hotels with separate rooms for the two of them. More than once she had had to resort to Airbnb in secret. Her father would never approve if he thought they were taking advantage of the "new economy," as he called it, but Jean Luc's "Maison Musique" had sounded too perfect to pass up—private, secluded, close to enough ancient burial grounds to satisfy her father's hunger for history and only forty euros for the two of them. She had told Papa it was a B&B and he had accepted her lie without comment.

Following the scribbled instructions, Ginny turned into a lane lined with climbing yellow roses and tall pink hollyhocks. She parked behind an ancient Mercedes and, leaving her father in the car, slid out and went up to the front door of a white farmhouse and rapped. She could hear a television inside. There were dead leaves on the narrow steps and a pile of oily rags and automotive tools, which made her wonder if her reservation had been clear—did Jean Luc know they were coming? She had not actually talked to him, just sent a text, in English. She rapped again, then stepped back so abruptly as the door flew open she almost lost her footing.

A man reached out and steadied her. Jean Luc was tall, about her age, strong and plump with cropped white hair and round blue eyes that brimmed with welcome. Ginny, never one to linger in matters of the heart, promptly fell in love, but regaining her balance was still able to say, *"Parlez vous anglais?"*

Jean Luc's grin as he shook his head No was so joyous that Ginny grinned back, barely able to stifle the deep silent laugh that had started to roll and echo inside her. This always happened when she met someone totally wrong for her, but it hadn't happened in years and she had almost given up. Still smiling, she explained that she did not speak much French. "But my father…" she gestured toward the parked car. "He will be able to talk to you."

"You will not talk to me?"

"I will try."

"Yes? Inside, please. Wine? Yes?"

"I would love a glass of wine," Ginny agreed. "But my father? Asleep in the car?"

"He is not happy there?"

Ginny glanced behind her as Jean Luc drew her into the house; Papa might not be happy, but he was perfectly safe in the shade by the fence hung with roses. And the house seemed safe too, clean and modern, with a wall of bright family photographs. Nor did there seem to be anything to fear in Jean Luc. He was a clown. Barefoot, his large white legs in rumpled red shorts, he was walking backwards so he could continue to beam at her. What did he see? She was fifty-three years old, for God's sake. She taught in an inner-city school and sang in a church choir. Her hair was badly dyed, her nose was peeling from yesterday's cemetery sunburn, her jeans were baggy and her breath stank. She beamed back.

"I see you like American music," she said, nodding toward the familiar face on his tee-shirt.

"You know Frank Zappa?" He clapped both hands over his heart. "I love Frank Zappa." He paused, his blue eyes troubled. "I do not," he offered, "like Neil Diamond."

"No one likes Neil Diamond."

"Oh. Ah. Ha ha. Thank you. You will sit?" He gestured toward a kitchen stool by the counter and patted his heart again.

"I should probably see the bedrooms first," Ginny said.

"Of course. But first." He opened the refrigerator that, except for a half dozen bottles of wine, was empty, pulled out a bottle, poured her a glass, and watched worriedly as she took a sip. The wine was too sweet, like Jean Luc himself, but she took another sip to assure him. Haltingly, as he settled, eyes luminous, on the stool opposite her, she began to ask him questions about himself. She could not be sure of all the answers but it seemed that he lived alone, had just recently started to rent out rooms, had left some sort of engineering job—trouble with a co-worker? a supervisor?—she couldn't tell. He played ping pong, did she know ping pong? He was a ping pong King Kong! Did she want to see his gold cups? No, of course not, why would she, they were not real gold, ha ha. More wine? Would she like to see what he kept in the closet over there? Look! Drums! A keyboard! Saxophones! And a guitar, yes, he played, no, not like Frank Zappa, maybe some day, but…. "I show you, please?" He settled down on a hassock and played a ballad, which he sang to her, in French, blushing furiously all the while.

The familiar tap of the cane as her father came into the house made them both look up. The old man studied Jean Luc, who rose with a clatter and an outstretched hand. "Loopy de Loop," Ginny's father decided, under his breath, and then, turning to Ginny, "Drinking?"

"It's some sort of dessert wine is all," Ginny said.

Jean Luc continued holding out his hand and her father continued to ignore it. There followed a short exchange in French between the two of them, which sounded pleasant enough, Ginny thought, and then Jean Luc led them upstairs to the bedrooms. A not very clean bathroom with the toilet seat up occupied the first landing, and Ginny's heart sank, but another short flight led to two large airy rooms overlooking an orchard. Jean Luc moved to pull the door shut on a third room containing a rumpled futon and a computer desk overflowing with piles of laundry. "I do not expect you so soon," he apologized.

"Soon? We would have been here hours ago if my daughter hadn't braked for every wildflower. It's almost seven o'clock. We need to eat. Can you tell us where to go?" Ginny listened as her father asked again in French and Jean Luc answered gravely, looking so stricken that once again Ginny felt a giggle bubble up. "He says the only restaurant is miles away," Ginny's father translated. "And he wants to come with us."

"I will drive?" Jean Luc offered, leaning toward them, hands clasped, eager.

"Better you than she," Ginny's father agreed. "She's been drinking."

Jean Luc, looking from one to the other, asked, "Is all right?"

Ginny's father, stumping downstairs, said nothing, but Ginny nodded. "Yes, it's all right."

"I will have bath first." He studied her face, worried. "You will not go away?"

"I won't go away." Ginny couldn't help it. She laughed out loud.

Still laughing, she followed her father down to the kitchen and sat beside him at a little table while he studied the map for their route tomorrow. They were going to drive to Paris, visit Napoleon's tomb, see the Museum of the Resistance and the Memorial to the Deported, all of which she knew were going to depress her deeply, and then they were going to fly to London to see the Churchill War Rooms, which, being underground, would be sure to depress her even more. She patted her father's shoulder, finished her wine, and went out to the car to bring their luggage in. She heard Jean Luc whistling from the bathroom upstairs and stooped to pet a black cat that lay curled under a trellis. A pen of fat red hens clucked by the shade of an old barn and the apples in the orchard were almost ripe. She took a deep sniff of the yellow roses, wishing they were going to Giverny tomorrow instead of the Bastille but…next time. Her two favorite words. Next time she would go to Giverny with Jean Luc and they would marry in Ste. Chapelle and honeymoon on the Riviera. That's how time in France should be spent. She straightened, hoisted the two suitcases, and went back inside, pausing to study the photos on the wall. None of Jean Luc with a woman. One brunette with red lipstick was attractive but looked too much like Jean Luc to be a wife—maybe a sister?

The restaurant that Jean Luc, freshly bathed and reeking of cologne, drove them to in his twenty-year-old Mercedes was a beer garden in a strip mall about fifteen miles away, crowded with young people and loud with canned music. Ginny's father took one look, turned his hearing aid off, ordered a steak and a coffee, and proceeded to eat. "He's a history buff," Ginny explained to Jean Luc, who listened intently but looked so troubled she was not sure what, if anything, he understood. "He loves war. No one knows why. He grew up in Quebec and none of his relatives were soldiers. He never served in any army. But when we moved to the States my mother toured the Revolutionary War sites with him, and later my stepmother went to all the Civil War battlefields, and now it's my turn. He's having a ball," she added unconvincingly, cutting into her salad and taking a sip of the amber-colored beer that Jean Luc had told her was brewed here. Both were delicious.

Jean Luc touched his pink lips with his napkin. "The war… for me, as a child, in Normandy?" Leaning forward to catch his meaning, Ginny seemed to understand that his family went to the beaches of Saint Laurent in the summer, where he and his cousins swam in tide-filled craters left by the bombs that were warm as hot tubs. They collected shrapnel and shell casings and dove through the wrecks of war ships. "We find treasure," Jean Luc continued. "No gold. No jewels. But *coques et moules*, we bring home to my aunt to prepare with butter and garlic." He patted his stomach. "Delicious."

"Children," Ginny's father scolded, looking at the two of them as they laughed. He asked Jean Luc something in French and Ginny saw Jean Luc's blue eyes become instantly somber. She finished her beer as the conversation went on and waited for her father to translate for her. "His great uncle," her father said, reaching for his cane, "was gassed in World War One and his grandfather was shell shocked in World War Two. So it wasn't all fun and games."

"No one said it was, Papa."

"Watch yourself."

Her father rose to go to the men's room and Ginny, chastised, waited until he was gone to meet Jean Luc's eyes. "My father wishes I was a more serious person. He actually thinks I'm a…" she began, then stopped, frustrated by her lack of French. Why had she never learned any language but Latin! Who could you speak to in Latin? Was "flibbertigibbet" even a word in Latin? Probably not. And why had her father decided, years ago, that she was one?

"He tells me you have many husbands," Jean Luc prompted.

"Yes." Ginny grimaced and held up three fingers. "No children. And you?"

Jean Luc fixed her with his blue eyes and moved his ringless hand back and forth across the tablecloth. "I have a special life," he said.

Ginny, warned (but of what?), sat back. When the check came her father paid it, overriding Jean Luc's protests. "Don't bother," her father told him, adding, unnecessarily and, Ginny hoped, incomprehensibly, "I always end up paying for my daughter's men."

Jean Luc's touch on her back as they went out into the parking lot was warm and light. She was quiet in the back seat as the two men talked, looking out at the dark fields. She had read in one of her father's books that more than 16,000 civilians had been killed by bombs in this part of France before it was "liberated." All that death and mess and misery, and for what? For her? So she could be an entitled peacetime princess bearing an old man's insults? What was he so bitter about? It was true her father had helped her out after her last divorce, but she had paid him back. She had always paid him back. He just wanted to fight. Well, tough. She wasn't a fighter. Never had been. The old man was going to have to deal with his bad temper and his bad manners on his own. No wonder he liked war! Tired, Ginny leaned her head against the seat and when Jean Luc glanced over his shoulder to smile at her, she smiled back.

In bed that night, listening to the frogs from the pond below her window, she wondered what she would do if Jean Luc were to appear in her doorway—but of course he would not. It would be up to her to go to him. She thought back to the walk they had taken through the orchard after her father retired. Jean Luc had led her past the chicken coop and the barn to the old stables that he planned to turn into a concert hall. He had many friends, he'd told her, talented musicians, and people would come from all over Europe to hear them. Looking in at the abandoned animal stalls cluttered with tools, Ginny had said nothing. Every man she'd ever loved had had a dream as foolish as this. She could not believe she had come all the way to France only to meet someone so completely her type—lonely, naïve, hopeful, self-absorbed, and useless. Where did these men come from? And why did they always end up breaking her heart? She had turned to go back to the house and Jean Luc had followed, head down, but then, at the door, he had turned her around and kissed her. A clumsy kiss, half on her nose, half on her cheek, but sweet, so sweet she was still thrilled by it.

Ginny slipped out of bed. Her father's bedroom light was out; he would be asleep by now, hearing aid off. She tiptoed into the bathroom, where the toilet seat was down, the floor had been mopped, fresh towels lay on the counter, and there was an opened bottle of bubble bath—Jean Luc used bubble bath!—on the rim of the tub. She giggled, peed, did the ritual stare in the mirror she always did before making a decision, turned toward her bedroom, rethought her decision, returned to her bedroom to pull a condom out of her purse, and went into Jean Luc's room.

It was like having sex with a puppy. Their lovemaking was quiet but surprisingly rowdy. Ginny was sniffed and snuffled and tickled and licked and patted and petted into a state of floating pleasure, but returning to her own bed just before dawn, she was fairly certain she had not actually been penetrated. Not that it mattered. She felt replete. The beginnings of love were the ones she loved best, before the lover became depressed or needy or—like her last husband—abusive.

Her father roused her in the morning with a sharp knock on her bedroom door. Throwing on her clothes and packing hurriedly, she met him at the foot of the stairs; he was packed and ready to leave. "Your boyfriend's still asleep," he said. "You must have worn him out last night."

"I don't know what you're talking about," Ginny said automatically, following him out to the car with the two suitcases. "And he's not my boyfriend."

"He's someone's," her father said, settling into the seat beside her and buckling up. "Did you see the photo of him on the wall? Red lipstick and a wig. You sure do find them, Virginia Jane."

"Oh, you know what, Papa? I forgot something. Just a sec." Going back into the house, Ginny bent to recheck the photo of the brunette on the wall—yes, that was Jean Luc all right, in drag. Oh my. She reached for the guest book on the table, scrawled her email address on a blank page, brushed a tear off her cheek, and wrote, "Next time." Then she went back to the car, got in beside her father, turned the key and backed out the lane to the street. She had only gone half a block when she looked in the rearview mirror and saw Jean Luc, barefoot and in his red shorts, chasing after them. Plump, breathless, he held a spray of yellow roses in one hand and a basket of eggs in the other.

"Keep going," her father said, but she had already stopped, turned the motor off, and unrolled her window as Jean Luc leaned in, panting. "For you," he said, handing her father the basket. "And for you," he said, giving Ginny the roses. Another damp, sweet, off-center kiss and he stepped back and waved.

After a few miles her father spoke. "What are we going to do with a dozen raw eggs?" he asked.

"I don't know, Papa. Food fight?"

Her father said nothing but she saw him bite back a smile. Smiling herself, Ginny turned onto the freeway and headed for Paris, her lap filled with roses.

Jon Ching, *Flowers in Her Hair*, 2016, oil on wood, 14 × 11 inches

Masculinities

Paul Strohm

SAILOR DOLL

My father was edgy about my Christmas request for a doll. "Gol-darnit," he was saying to my mother, "where does that kid get his ideas?" What was the problem? My sister had a dozen and I was only asking for one. Innocent of the role of sailors in the gay imagination, he decided the answer was to get me a sailor doll. I named him "Petey." The first thing I did was shrink his wool uniform in my sister's doll washing machine. I took him to school anyway, for show and tell, unclad except for pinched-looking little black sailor oxfords.

FOOTBALLER

Ever hopeful, my father bought me a kid-sized football uniform, complete with ungainly plastic shoulder pads and an ear-crunching, vision-obscuring helmet. He dressed me up in it and sent me down to the vacant lot where the neighborhood kids ran a pickup game. Briefly awed by my official-looking getup, they abandoned previous custom and handed me the ball. For a long five or six seconds all of us stood there, frozen, wondering whether my costume had trans-formed me into a credible athlete. Then they recollected themselves, unceremoniously threw me to the ground, and punched away any thought of equipment-based advantage.

SOME CAR

I meant to buy a practical sedan. I came home with a mean-looking Chevy Camaro instead. Not much of a back seat, but the children were still small. I settled for the six-cylinder model. "Some car," my friends said. "Like Paul," my wife said. "Looks good but not much under the hood." No wonder that marriage didn't last. My next car was a Prelude, also low slung. Claire was sitting in it at the gas station. She became convinced that a guy was hanging around and ogling her. I gave him a look. He said, "You wanna sell that car?"

BIKER

Unchained country dogs always went after Ray: snarled, nipped at him in passing, reluctantly fell away. Because he was always out front, toiling, they considered him leader of our two-man pack. Or maybe the opposite: viewed him as the weak link, sensed in him some sweat-drenched vulnerability. Ray was a pessimist, always braced for a bad outcome. His biggest gripe was about hills, at least the downhill kind. "Uh-oh," he'd say, when we came to one. Starting a downhill swoop, rather than enjoy the effortless movement, he'd imagine the climb ahead. "This'll cost us," he'd mutter. "We'll pay for this."

WEDDING CHINA

Exasperated with our failing marriage, my wife expressed herself by breaking dishes. She'd go in after dinner, wash a few, and then: zing! crash!—a plate would hit the floor. Our registered "wedding china"—Dansk Spisa Ribb—was going fast. After the divorce I housesat for a friend whose kitchen was stocked with the same pattern. One morning I was asleep upstairs when my still-angry wife staged a home invasion. Whatever her objective, upon entering the kitchen by the screen door she spied this new trove. I was awakened by the familiar sound: Spisa Ribb shattering on tiled floor.

AMONG MEN

I drove up to Point Arena to see about seafood. Out on the pier some seasoned-looking guys were bringing in rockfish, still flopping around and with goggley eyes. They sold me a couple, at a tourist price, but I was enjoying the camaraderie. I hovered while they spouted various extreme views, complaining about things like chickenshits who wanted to turn the Point into a marine sanctuary. When I came off the pier a guy asked me, "What're you catching?" I said, kinda casually, "Rockfish." He said, "How deep?" "Actually," I confessed, "I bought these." He brushed past, averting his gaze.

FORMIDABLE MEMBER

Claire is telling me about the Writers' Colony, where she hung around with an eminent poet. It seems that he has a formidable member. That's a line of thought I'd rather not pursue, or anyway it evokes a succession of images I can do without. I don't know much about writers' colonies, except of course for their legendary promiscuity. But this one is also known for its spontaneous events, like midnight swims. Maybe that's where she got a look at this guy's equipment. "So you met him on one of those midnight swims?" I suggest. "No," she says, "not really…."

TWO-SHARK

Carolyn and I were fly-fishing in the Florida Keys. As novices, we had a guide. We were after tarpon and bonefish, but they weren't running. The guide suggested we go for shark instead. He started throwing bloody chum in the water and sharks gathered around the little flat-bottomed boat. I caught one right away and then Carolyn followed up by catching two. You get a nickname on a fishing trip. On land everybody started calling her "Two-Shark." Oh, I had a name too, but based on a snack item I had brought along: "Mr. Peanut." Not quite the same, somehow.

Mark Ropers, *Bound for Kilkenney Beach*, 2016, watercolor, 11 × 13 inches

Douglas Iris

Dave Seter

In their camaraderie irises talk
underground in hormones and iron.
I stop before the solitary one to try
to understand its petal tongue.

There's an advantage to knowing a friend
or a flower—but I've seen their heads nod
just the same when we talk—and wonder
which is distracted, which understands?

It's curious some life forms root
to the spot, others are doomed to wander.
The iris won't choose to live with us
but may be cut and (briefly) possessed.

Looking in its eye you may say beauty—
no mirror nearby for it to argue the point—
and no small talk—only the burst of perfume
it takes going down on one knee to know well.

Mary K. Shisler, *Wabi Sabi Tulips*,
2016, archival print

Waiting for a Target

Bogside Remembered

Richard Kirschman

No Man's Land

———

IN THE SUMMER of 1969, I was traveling through Northern Ireland as a tourist. These photographs were taken in August in the Catholic Bogside District of Londonderry. The occasion was the annual Apprentice Boys Parade, in remembrance of the Protestant Loyal Order that slammed the doors on the army of the Catholic King James in 1689.

Tensions had been building in the city for more than a year over Protestant control in a majority Catholic and nationalist population. The Apprentice Boys Parade was an annual affront to the Catholic neighborhoods they marched through with their banners flying and bagpipes blaring.

Police Throwing Rocks

———

The marchers were just turning the corner of the Bogside when a man standing to my right threw a rock into their midst. Within minutes, the parade turned into a riot, which further deteriorated over the next few days into a pitched street battle between the largely Catholic residents of the Bogside and the B Specials, a mostly Protestant Police Auxiliary.

Throughout the battle recorded here, I was able to move freely through the no man's land that lay between the barricades, using my not-exactly-legitimate *Ramparts* press credential. To anyone who asked from either side, I said, "Don't you want your side of the story told?" and the police—or a Bogside neighbor—would call out, "Hold it, boys! Let him cross!"

Watching the Bogside Burn

There were no guns, only clubs, stones, hoses, and Molotov cocktails. During these first few days, people acted openly. There was no attempt to conceal actions or mask identities. Three years later, the Bogside Massacre, also known as Bloody Sunday, occurred in the same neighborhood, when British soldiers shot twenty-six unarmed civilians during a peaceful protest march. Fourteen people died. Bloody Sunday was one of the most significant events of "the Troubles" because a large number of civilians were killed by forces of the state in full view of the public and the press. This was the largest number of people killed in a single shooting incident during the conflict.

Open Mic

San Rafael, California

Robin Leslie Jacobson

The weatherman hasn't seen anything like it
in the twenty years he's been on the radio—
first rain of the fall, storm winds pinwheeling
from Santa Rosa to San Jose.

We huddle in the front seat listening to blues
and bursts of static, water sheeting down the windows
like hard spray from a carwash. The rain
shows no sign of letting up, so we make a run for it,
splash through the river sluicing down the storm drain.

And the weather lurches in with us, pulses off the walls
like house music.

Now I wish I'd brought something else to read.
No metaphors to towel me dry. Not even a simile,
merciful as shelter. On a night like this,
in a town where so many things are named for dead saints,

I want something fugitive and wild—
something that would change the weather
inside me as I spoke, split me the way lightning
splits a dead tree. A sound the rain couldn't drown out.
Char it couldn't wash away.

Patricia Connolly, *Late Afternoon at McInnis*, 2016, pastel, 6½ × 11½ inches

Bob Kubik, *Fox*, 2016, oil on wood panel, 7½ × 13¾ inches

Post-Election Walkabout

Brooke Williams

DAY 1   November 8, 2016. America elected Donald Trump as president.

DAY 2   My wife, the writer Terry Tempest Williams, and I took a morning walk along the Colorado River running by the lodge where we'd spent the night after watching the election returns.

Like most progressives, we'd been confident that Hillary would be our next president. Since few residents of Castle Valley, Utah own a television, we had reserved a large room at a lodge on the Colorado River and invited our friends to watch the election returns. Everyone brought food and drink. The party-like atmosphere with which the evening began dissipated once the polls closed, and within an hour a paralytic gas had filled the room. Half our group noticed it early and escaped. One by one the others slipped out quietly and by 10:00 p.m., only three of us remained. We could not move. We could not move until Day 2's sun flooded the room.

After our walk we went home. I cleaned out a storage room which, since we moved in in 1999, had been visited only by wood rats, snakes, and black widow spiders.

DAY 3   I filled my backpack and walked off our porch, across our field, and through the gate, where I stopped to tighten my boots. Without knowing it, I also dropped the pens I'd planned on using to make sense of what happened and, I hoped, make a plan for what

I might do about it. Then I walked across the section of Bureau of Land Management land just outside our gate, crossed through the culvert beneath the LaSal Mountain Road, and wandered out into the wilderness.

When I came back three days later I started writing what I could remember about my journey. When I stopped I had fifty single-spaced pages. What follows describes my first night, after a rugged day of climbing in and out of deep washes, finding my way between boulders the size of small houses, dodging pour offs, and struggling up steep, soft sand, often stunned by the wild beauty.

I'd found a perfect camp spot perched between two minor washes at the base of an ancient juniper. This section begins after I'd eaten dinner.

When I'd finished my *Tasty Bite* Pad Thai, I poured a few ounces of the still-steamy water into the plastic measuring cup I use for a dish and swirled it around, until the remnants became suspended in the then soup-like liquid. Which I then drank, as if I knew how precious water was about to become.

Clicking on my headlamp, I was sick about my missing pens, inclined as I was to make notes about where I was, how I got there, and why it all made sense. As if until I wrote it down, nothing would make sense. Plus, I've learned not to wait for insights to force me to pen and paper, but to pull out pen and paper and see what gets written down.

I unfolded my map. Since I couldn't mark it, I needed to memorize my route and also where I thought I was camped. As is typical in these canyons, the map in no way represented the actual terrain I'd spent the previous four hours crossing. Topographers using aerial photographs cannot capture all the intrigue possible within forty-foot contours. On the map I followed my route across the four blue-veined gorges fed by Adobe Mesa between where I dropped into the main drainage and where I felt sure I was camped. There, in the warm comfort of my seat and the moon's soft presence, I ignored what the map showed I would face in the morning.

I read in the light of my headlamp, cozy in my miraculous parka, a stocking cap, and gloves.

Terry had given me my new parka a month before—an early Christmas present. This wasn't just any parka, but a Patagonia Fitz Roy down (made from *Traceable Down: 800-fill-power goose down from geese traced from parent farm to apparel factory to help ensure the birds that supply it are not force-fed or live-plucked*) parka. Although designed for serious alpine climbers, this parka had become my most prized possession.

I am anything but a serious alpine climber. I am, however, a committed wilderness explorer. You won't find photos of me in my new parka in a dogsled documenting bird migration across Antarctica. Or in shorts and sandals in a dugout canoe mapping a tributary of the Amazon River. The wilderness I explore is vastly internal. This might have to do with my age (sixty-four) and my withering interest in the physical risks and time commitment my previous obsessions with powder skiing, canyoneering, and climbing required. But I'm also feeling "called."

While there are many ways into this inner wilderness, for me the most effective access is through the outer wilderness—during a quiet, solitary walk in a familiar redrock canyon, or looking up through the universe on a moonless desert night, perched on a ridge watching a long view. Or sitting in a camp chair in the winter desert awed watching cliff light pass through the entire spectrum of red.

Awe is the quickest, most direct route into that caldron of evolution we all have simmering deep inside us, whether or not we're aware of it. We're taught to ignore it, this "id" that Freud thought needed to be contained if society were to function smoothly, seamlessly.

This is the "core" biological human, that "secret person, undamaged" in each of us, according to Human Ecologist Paul Shepard. Awe punctures any shell society has deposited over our true selves and, I believe, fires up evolution. Over the past year, I'd discovered the work of a Berkeley psychologist, Dacher Keltner, who has quantified the "pro-social" behavior associated with awe. In other words, experiencing awe encourages us to contribute to the collective good of our species.

Terry had made a very conscious purchase when she chose that parka. Would it work exploring the inner wilderness when it was designed specifically for the outer wilderness?

A stiff breeze moved past me from behind, pushing the light ahead of it. I pulled up the heavy-duty zipper shielded beneath the down-filled tubes, sealing it against any cold. Then over my hat, I pulled on the hood, specially designed to keep even the back of my neck warm. I was ready.

Shepard wrote that the "mind expanded with the vista," referring to evolution and ancestors' increasing brain size when they climbed down from the trees and wandered out onto the savannah. Anyone who has gazed out at an infinite view has experienced this expansion on an individual level. I felt it that evening: cliffs and sky no matter which way I turned. Thank goodness my hood was designed to cover a climbing helmet and therefore had room for such expansion.

Terry knows that while I still love getting out and scrambling in the rocks and cracks, I've become more contemplative, more motivated to wander around with no destination or to sit and watch time unfurl in front of me. She shares my new knowledge that tapping into the deeper and possibly sacred dimensions of wild places requires stillness. She was considering all this while shopping for my new parka. Her main objective: a parka that would keep me warm and dry when I wasn't exerting any physical effort.

Although the description of my parka did not include the phrase, *for those deep winter days wandering aimlessly in the desert, or perched in the sand in freezing air watching the long view,* she thought it could have. Not only would my new parka be perfect for what was fast becoming my preferred outdoor activity, having it would encourage me to be out on the even coldest, darkest days, when staying in would sink my mood.

My belly full and the sun gone and the last weak light suddenly consumed by blackness, I crawled into my sleeping bag.

No sound makes its own sound, I thought. Then I wondered if, like birds and wildflowers, silence exists in many forms. True silence is not the absence of sound, but the absence of distraction. I lay there in the growing moonlight (a few days from full, when the supermoon would be closer to Earth than it has been for fifty years), paying attention to the different forms of silence. First, I felt throbbing—I did not hear it—a slow pulsing. I wondered if the source of this throbbing was my heart moving blood around inside of me or outside, all around me. The harder I listened the more this feeling turned to sound. "Thrumming" is the closest word I have to describe it. This thrumming gave way to vibrations I swear I could both hear and feel beneath me, and I wondered if the source of this silence was deep in the earth, and if paying more attention to it brought it closer to the surface.

My weariness no match for the full force of the moon, I gave in and drifted off. I fell asleep as the vibrations turned to buzzing, as if power was moving all around me.

I woke up a few hours later, recalling the dreaming but not the dream, hours during which Donald Trump had not crossed my mind.

Swimming Through Summer

Judy Brackett

On endless summer afternoons,
we set out to swim through the fields
toward the ends of the Earth,
maybe walk partway on our hands
as our father liked to do—
      pennies, nickels, dimes,
      cellophane-wrapped mints
      raining
      from his pockets,
      his pantlegs ruffling
      up to his knees—
and hours later we would wade our way home
to the long evenings, and he would try to teach us how—
      something like a frog squat,
      palms spread on the grass,
      knees propped on our upper arms/elbows,
      our legs slowly reaching for sky,
      and we'd wobble there a few dizzy moments
then we'd float through the twilight to supper, coins
jingling in our pockets, mints and clover
on our tongues, lightning-bug smears on our foreheads,
our heads damp-cloudy with downside-up wonders.

Cathy Rose, *Accept*, 2017, hand-formed porcelain and found materials, 7 × 14 × 6½ inches.
Courtesy of Seager Gray Gallery, Mill Valley, California

Ken

Gina Cloud

I'm trying hard to see
what it is
I'm looking at
before I tell myself
what it is
I'm looking at.

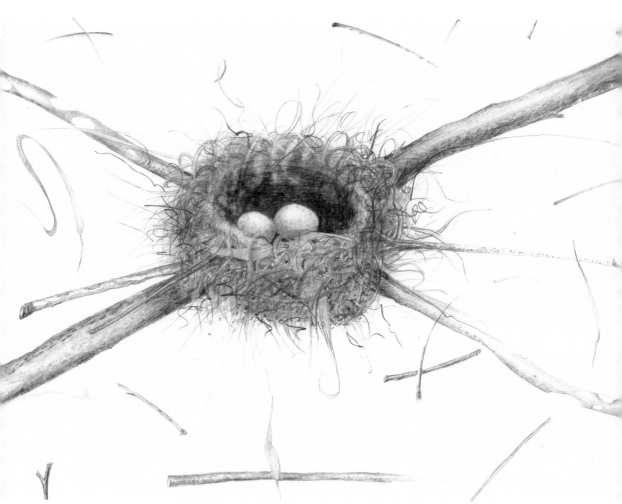

Anne Faught, *Coming Together*, 2015, graphite on paper, 18 × 24 inches

Writers and Artists

STEPHEN AJAY lives in Point Reyes Station with Anne and the saintly dogs, Finn and Leo. He has two books of poetry with New Rivers Press, *ABRACADABRA* and *The Whales Are Burning*. His poetry has appeared in *The Progressive*, *The Paris Review*, and *Ploughshares*, among other journals.

LILY ANDREWS is in Kindergarten at Bolinas-Stinson School. She loves the color purple, her little sister Ada, and working on her fairy garden.

Inspired by the Hubble Space Telescope photographs, JOHANNA BARUCH's abstract paintings reflect the beauty of the universe, a place where science and mystery intertwine. Her work is exhibited in galleries and museums, and is in private and corporate collections nationwide.

KAREN BENKE is the author of three creative writing adventure books from Shambhala Publications. A mother and teacher, she lives and works from The Writers' Nest in downtown Mill Valley, California.

PHILIP BONE works in Special Education and Outdoor Education. He is proud of an artistic heritage and progeny. Inspiration and recreation blend in the Sierra Nevada where he lives.

SOFIA BORG is thirteen years old and attends Bolinas-Stinson School. She is an aspiring ballet dancer, loves playing ukulele and being with her friends.

A New England transplant, KAY BRADNER paints and plays with grandchildren on a hill above the ocean in San Francisco.

DEBORAH BUCHANAN is a writer who lives in the shadow of the Oregon Coast Range, digging in the dirt between trips near and far.

CHRISTA BURGOYNE works in Berkeley and plays in West Marin.

GLENN CARTER, born in San Francisco, resides in Santa Cruz, California. First memory: light, sound, and mist of a waterfall. Observer, painter, and garden keeper.

NANCY CHERRY reports that she continues to write beside and within the boundaries of the Point Reyes National Seashore, but still hasn't nailed it. "That may never happen," she says, "but what's life without insurmountable challenges?"

Fascinated and inspired by the natural world, JON CHING paints in a tightly rendered manner to comment on the human experience, paying respect to the perfect intricacies of evolution.

RICH CLARKE was first enthralled with Kehoe Beach in the 1960s. It became the "Clarke family church" from then on. His photo speaks to that place's forever-comforting beach grass welcome.

Poet, playwright, and amateur historian GINA CLOUD lives near the coast of southern Sonoma County, California. She spends much time outdoors, finding revelation and logic that sustains and inspires her writing.

PATRICIA CONNOLLY lives in Fairfax, California and is a member of the Pastel Society of the West Coast. She works primarily in chalk pastel, focusing on impressions of the landscape.

Self-taught, born in France, living in Marin County, EMMELINE CRAIG created the Blissful Gallery in Stinson Beach, California, featuring her uplifting paintings, designed to quiet the mind and expand consciousness.

JUDY BRACKETT CROWE, a native of Nebraska, lives in the northern Sierra Nevada foothills of California. Her stories and poems have appeared in journals and anthologies from *About Place* to *Untidy Season*.

In her art practice, CHRISTEL DILLBOHNER looks closely at the natural world and the essentials of human existence. She is represented by Don Soker Contemporary Art in San Francisco.

TOBI EARNHEART-GOLD grew up in Bolinas, California. He still loves surfing there.

Writer and photographer JAUNE EVANS is a lifelong student of literature, art, nature, and religion. West Marin is a sacred place of wonder and friendships for her.

ANNE FAUGHT is a West Marin artist, gardener, and long distance walker. She has returned to her studio after years of teaching, delighted to be working and living in paradise.

KAITLYN GALLAGHER was raised on Richardson Bay in Sausalito, California. She is a high school and college English teacher, an essayist, poet, and novelist.

MOLLY GILES is the author of four prize-winning story collections and a novel. She still misses the office she once had over the Old Western Saloon in Point Reyes Station, but makes do writing from her home in Woodacre, California.

JANI GILLETTE grew up in the Bay Area amidst redwoods, oaks, and Apple computer. Art and dance come together in her work, with a wink and a nod to whimsy.

ELIZABETH GOREK paints women occupied with their own thoughts and sensations, facing their own direction, and happily unaware of observation.

SUSAN HALL's recent book, *River Flowing Home: A Creative Journey*, is the story of her odyssey from West Marin to New York City, where she exhibited her work in galleries and museums for more than twenty years. In the early 1990s she returned to live and work in West Marin, the source of her inspiration.

KIMBERLY CARR HARMON is a photographer living in Marin County. She draws inspiration from nature here and wandering the English countryside. "In this world of busy-ness, I choose to wander."

ROBERT HASS's most recent book of poems is *The Apple Trees at Olema*. Also new is *A Little Book on Form: An Exploration into the Formal Imagination of Poetry*. He lives in Inverness, California and is a professor of English at the University of California at Berkeley.

BARBARA HEENAN lives in Inverness, California. She began writing in the fourth grade when her teacher assigned the class a project to write and illustrate autobiographies. She has been writing off and on ever since.

TOM HICKEY is a writer living in London. He previously lived in Oakland and traveled to Point Reyes frequently.

A Bay Area painter dividing her time and inspiration between her hometown of Marshall, California and her studio in San Francisco, ISIS HOCKENOS studied art and writing at Sarah Lawrence College.

Calling on her training and experience in the arts and healing, ROBIN LESLIE JACOBSON teaches creative writing workshops with a focus on sensory awareness. She is a poetry coach, editor, and designer widely published and honored.

Born in Manhattan, RICHARD KIRSCHMAN has lived and thrived in the beauty and peace of western Marin County for more than forty years, as far from the world's religious violence as he can get.

MATTHEW POLVOROSA KLINE is an artist living in West Marin. His focus is on the ways of wildlife and nature while working in photography, film, and conservation.

BOB KUBIK is happy to have the time and freedom to do what he wishes. Having lived in many places, he is delighted to be in West Marin for the last chapter of his life.

TONI LITTLEJOHN is an artist whose paint shows up as a geological event. She has been leading art workshops for twenty-five years, is the Board President of Gallery Route One, and is a devotee of ping pong and swimming in Tomales Bay.

SHERRIE LOVLER is a painter and poet from Santa Rosa, California. The calligraphic line permeates her artwork. She is the author of *On Softer Ground: Paintings, Poems and Calligraphy*.

JACKIE GARCIA MANN is an East Bay mother of three teenagers. She has a background in wildlife ecology. For the past few years she has been amusing herself by writing short stories, personal essays, and poetry.

CAITLIN MCCAFFREY is an artist whose commercial photography has appeared in numerous publications and whose fine art has been exhibited widely. She works alongside her long-toothed, wide-eared handsome hound in Sonoma County.

Now living in Davis, California, G. DAVID MILLER is a consultant to international development organizations in Asia, Africa, and the Middle East. He was one of the founders of the *West Marin Review*.

LISSA NICOLAUS grew up in Carmel, California and resides in Marin County. Her impressionistic oil paintings capture dramatic beaches, rolling hills, waterfront vistas, farms, and villages. Lissa is a founding member of BayWood Artists. Her work was featured in *Plein Air Magazine* in 2015.

LISA PIAZZA lives in Oakland, California with her two daughters. Her stories and poems appear in various publications, including *Cicada*; *Brain, Child*; and *Cosmonauts Avenue*.

SUSAN PUTNAM, once a practicing research biochemist, gave up science to practice art. Her mediums include charcoal, pastel, crayon, and gouache. She lives in San Rafael, California.

CYNTHIA FONTAINE REEHL lives outside of Boston with her family and their Cavalier King Charles Spaniel, Riley Coyote. She worked in publishing for many years and is now writing a novel.

JULIA EDITH RIGBY is a painter, print-maker, and illustrator living in Petaluma, California. Her work explores wildness and wild things, in particular the flora and fauna of coastal California.

MARK ROPERS is an Inverness watercolorist and member of Point Reyes Open Studios. He is interested in presenting thoughtful, mood-evoking paintings of landscapes, water-related pleasures, and objects of interest.

CATHY ROSE has been a figurative mixed-media artist for more than twenty years. She owns Lucky Rose Gallery in the historic New Orleans French Quarter, featuring her porcelain, clay, wood, and found-object sculptures.

BARRY ROTH is a biologist, editor, and poet. He lives in San Francisco.

MARIUS SALONE is thirteen and attends Bolinas-Stinson school. He is passionate about fashion and skateboarding. Every day Marius loves to plan new outfits to wear. He also is very excited about continuing his art career.

PRARTHO SERENO's most recent poetry collection is *Elephant Raga*. She teaches at the College of Marin, is a Poet in the Schools, and was the fourth Poet Laureate of Marin.

DAVE SETER is a civil engineer and poet. Born in Chicago, he now lives in Petaluma, California. His poetry and critical work have recently appeared in *Paterson Literary Review*, *Asheville Poetry Review*, and *Confluence*.

MARY K. SHISLER is an Oakland-based artist who adores botany. Born and raised in Wisconsin, she moved to California twenty years ago. She has taught photography in many venues and has shown her art work internationally.

MARY SIEDMAN has lived on the mesa in Bolinas, California for nearly forty years. As a painter, she concentrates on exposing the light and movement of her natural surroundings.

It has been DAVE STAMEY's life's work to celebrate the rural American West. He has recorded eleven albums of original music, traveled hundreds of thousands of miles, and performed thousands of shows doing just that. He lives in the farthest northeastern corner of Tulare County, California. The foothills of the Sierra Nevada Mountains begin just outside his back door.

PAUL STROHM is emeritus professor of the humanities at Columbia University and life fellow of St. Anne's College, Oxford. He divides his time between Brooklyn, New York and Oxford, England.

DAVID SWAIN was born in Ohio, grew up near Boston, and has lived in the Bay Area for more than thirty years. An earlier poem, "Witness," appeared in Volume 2 of the *West Marin Review*.

MICHAEL SYKES lived in Inverness, California for twenty-seven years before moving to California's high northeastern desert in 1994. There he owns a bookstore and publishes under the imprint of Floating Island Publications, with fifty-four titles in print.

Born in rural Quảng Ngãi Province, Vietnam, MAY TA's illustrations draw on memories of her childhood. "I remember things that people don't recall, and melancholy enshrouds my mind with things a child should not have seen. Drawing is a way of healing and connecting with the world."

JOAN THORNTON is a painter, writer, and a maker of artist's books. The surreal aspect of contemporary experience influences her creative output.

AMANDA TOMLIN is a medium- and large-format photographer who uses non-traditional techniques, including some from the 19th century, to print her negatives.

SATCHEL TRIVELPIECE is a fifth grader at the Bolinas-Stinson School.

MICHEL VENGHIATTIS has lived in West Marin since 1974. He grew up hearing a lot of stories from his parents about their experiences as members of the French Resistance.

VAN WARING grew up in California's Central Valley, but has since called West Marin her home. Her work has been spotted on all sorts of local walls. When she is not mind-mapping and scribbling, she finds order in the task of organizing and shelving books in various locations around town.

XANDER WEAVER-SCULL uses art to remind viewers of our intimate connection with all life on this planet and that our collective futures are bound together.

SANDY WHITE earned a BFA from the University of Pennsylvania and the Pennsylvania Academy of Fine Arts. She is a painter, poet, and bookkeeper living in Woodacre, California with four cats and a feral visitor.

BROOKE WILLIAMS's life has been one of adventure and wilderness exploration. His conservation career spans thirty years. His most recent book, *Open Midnight*, documents his exploration of places where outer and inner wilderness meet.

MARY WINEGARDEN taught at San Francisco State University and is a member of the Squaw Valley Community of Writers. Her first book, *The Translator's Sister*, won an American Book Award; recent poems have appeared in various journals. Along with swimming, grand-mothering, and protesting, she is working on new poems.

ARIEL WISH was born and currently resides in Burlington, Vermont. An aspiring writer, she is studying English and creative writing as an undergraduate at Saint Michael's College.

west marin review

Many Thanks to Our Donors

Lucid Art Foundation
Marin Poetry Center
West Marin Fund
Stephen Ajay
Lorraine Almeida
Carole Ballachey
Peter Barnes
Nancy Bertelsen
Deborah Buchanan
Wendy Friefeld
Kaitlyn Gallagher

Eugene Gregor
Johanna Immerman
Claudia Kopkowski
Bernard Krause
Jonathan Langdon
Rick Lyttle
David & Susan Miller
Julie Monson
Lissa Nicolaus
John Parman & Kathryn
Snowden Parman
Susan & John Putnam

Cynthia Fontaine Reehl
Meredith Sabini
Judith Shaw
Dean Shillinger
Carole Sirulnick
J.C. Stock
George Taylor
John & Pamela
Thompson
Matthew Werdegar
Carol Whitman &
Bob Kubik

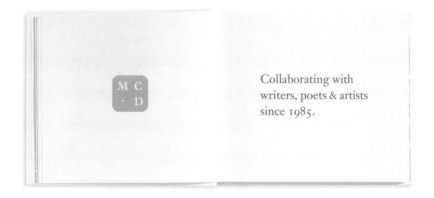

Collaborating with
writers, poets & artists
since 1985.

KWMR is a listener-supported community radio station and a beacon of locally produced INDEPENDENT MEDIA.

You can keep the signal strong, and support us today.
Visit KWMR.org.

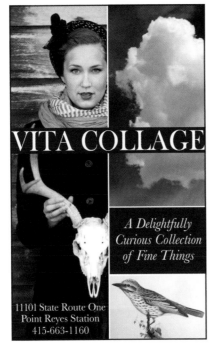

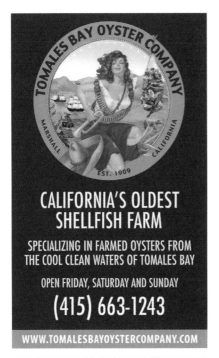

About the *West Marin Review*

West Marin Review
Volume 8, 2018

ISBN 978-0-9822829-7-7
Copyright ©2018 *West Marin Review*
All works copyright by and courtesy
of the artists and authors, unless
otherwise noted.

The *West Marin Review* is a publishing
collaboration among Neighbors & Friends
(Myn Adess, Madeleine Corson, Doris
Ober), Point Reyes Books (Stephen Sparks
and Molly Parent), Black Mountain Circle
(Steve Costa and Kate Levinson).

Prose Reviewers

Myn Adess	Claire Peaslee
Patricia Holt	James Shrieve
Doris Ober	

Poetry Reviewers

Willow Banks	Keith Ekiss
Lilyana Bone	James Shrieve
Madeleine Corson	

Art Reviewers

Lilyana Bone	Thomas Heinser
Madeleine Corson	Maxine Ressler

Volunteers

Dave Brast	Jan Langdon
Loretta Farley	Christina Waldeck
Bob Kubik	

*Special thanks to the following
local teachers:*

Ron Brown	Jason Richardson,
Kathy Bustamante	*Principal, Bolinas-*
Brian Kirven	*Stinson School*
Nuria Martinez-Lee	Janis Yerington

Managing Editor: Doris Ober
Associate Editor: Myn Adess
Design: Madeleine Corson, Lilyana Bone,
    with Maxine Ressler/corsondesign.com
General Manager/Advertising: Kamala Tully
Bookkeeping: Cathryn Irving
Proofreading: Myn Adess, Willow Banks,
    Suzanna Henderson, Patricia Holt,
    Arline Matheson, Doris Ober
Distributor: PGW

SUBMISSIONS
Submission guidelines: westmarinreview.org
or info@westmarinreview.org

SUPPORT THE *WEST MARIN REVIEW*
The *West Marin Review* is created through
the volunteer efforts of friends, neighbors,
artists, and writers. Donations are appreciated
(and tax deductible). To make a donation,
please visit westmarinreview.org.

West Marin Review
Post Office Box 1302
Point Reyes Station, California 94956
westmarinreview.org

BACK COVER Cathy Rose, *Balance*, 2013,
hand-formed porcelain and found objects,
12 × 28 × 6 inches. Courtesy of Seager Gray
Gallery, Mill Valley, California